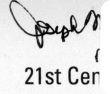

21st Cen

MW00769700

21st Century Mage

Bring the Divine Down to Earth

Jason Augustus Newcomb

WEISER BOOKS

Boston, MA/York Beach, ME

First published in 2002 by
Red Wheel/Weiser, LLC
York Beach, ME
With offices at:
368 Congress Street
Boston, MA 02210
www.redwheelweiser.com

Library of Congress Cataloging-in-Publication Data

Newcomb, Jason Augustus.
    21st century mage : bring the divine down to earth / by Jason Augustus
Newcomb.
        p. cm.
    Includes bibliographical references.
    ISBN 1-57863-237-4 (alk. paper)
    1. Magic. 2. Guardian angels—Miscellanea. 3. Abraham ben Simeon,
of Worms, 15th cent. I. Title: Twenty-first century mage. II. Title.
    BF1623.A53 N49 2002
    133.4'3—dc21

                                        2002001950

Typeset in Sabon, Univers Condensed, and Univers Extended

Printed in Canada
TCP

09 08 07 06 05 04 03 02
8 7 6 5 4 3 2 1

Table of Contents

Part III: Communion with the Divine

Introduction

Within the pages of this book you will find a complete elucidation of the most modern methods of illuminating your mind and achieving divine consciousness. Yet, these methods are based on some ancient practices for communing with your Holy Guardian Angel described in *The Sacred Magic of Abramelin the Mage*. I have distilled the widely variant methods for contacting the Holy Guardian Angel into a clear and concise plan, which I refer to as the Abramelin operation. You you can fashion this plan into your own unique spiritual practice. I have devoted my entire adult life to understanding the nature of the magical and religious experience, and I hope to share what I've learned in these pages.

I have always had an interest in spirituality, particularity the esoteric sort. Before my teens, I started to amass a small library of books on the occult, one of which happens to be *The Book of the Sacred Magic of Abramelin the Mage*. I consider myself a skeptical and pragmatic mystic. I love to experience the transcendent joy of higher states of consciousness and the oceanic experience of cosmic union, but I don't believe that mystical gadgets, crystals, and "secret knowledge" in and of themselves will get me there. Illumination is a natural state and requires neither special beliefs, psychedelic drugs, nor the "mercy" of God. God, whoever s/he really is, wants us to experience these ecstatic trances. S/he requires no sacrifices and no ascetic, behavioral taboos or moral strictures.

I spent my spiritual adolescence primarily within the Golden Dawn tradition, studying the teachings of its most famous student, Aleister Crowley. Virtually single-handedly, Crowley expanded the idea of the Holy Guardian Angel into the whole process of spiritual awakening.[1] In my experience, the Holy Guardian Angel is that completely divine part of you that is beyond waking consciousness. The experience of contacting your Holy Guardian Angel is the marriage of your "human being" with your "divine self"—your conscious self with your unconscious self. Uniting these two modes of consciousness has always been the goal of mystics and sages. It has sometimes been called the alchemical marriage of the Sun and the Moon or the marriage of the Red King and the White Queen. In Indian Tantric philosophy, it is often called the union of Shiva and Shakti. This union is said to take place in the spiritual third-eye center. All of these names and symbols reduce to the fact that illumination is one thing, regardless of the labels and explanations that people attach to it.

When I performed the Abramelin operation, I did many things wrong, omitted incredible amounts of the details of the operation as described in the *Abramelin*, and still managed to achieve the result I sought in much less time than the book prescribed. I feel that precisely following the instructions in any book is unnecessary, as long as you are consciously aware of your choices, and are following your personal intuition. I do, however, devote a chapter in this book to an outline of all the medieval rules for those of you who would like to follow the Abramelin plan to the letter.

In Part I, I outline the Abramelin operation so that you know what preparations to make. In Part II, I discuss the framework of your spiritual practice and methods you can use to develop it. Part III contains details about the culmination of your work—invoking your Holy Guardian Angel and working with it to positively transform your life.

I believe that profound spiritual experiences are the birthright of all human beings. These experiences awaken within us new and expanded possibilities for happiness, achievement, and wisdom. Many amazing and wonderful things have happened in my life as a direct result of working with the tools that I have outlined in this volume. I hope that you will experience similar joys.

Throughout history, there have been certain people— whether they are artists, mystics, religious leaders, or scientists—who were giant strides ahead of the rest of the human race. These people possessed a universal awareness, a super-conscious ability to see and create, and the wonders that they beheld and gave to the world have become the foundations of our cultures.

These people, whether they fully realized it or not, had created a connection with the universe that enabled them to see the "bigger picture" in ways that ordinary people only dream of. The theoretical physicist Albert Einstein; the mystics St.

Paul; Joan of Arc, and St. Teresa, the visionary occultist Aleister Crowley; the immortal playwright William Shakespeare; the nature-mystic-poet Walt Whitman; the founder of Christian Science, Mary Baker Eddy; the founder of the Theosophical Society, Helena P. Blavatsky; and many, many others throughout history possessed genius, vision, and unearthly imagination. These people had, in one way or another, the Knowledge and Conversation of their Holy Guardian Angels.

We all have this potential for power, genius, and vision. Every person has the potential for a universal awareness. Conversing with the Holy Guardian Angel is a mode of access to the connection between human consciousness and universal, or divine, consciousness. We are all born with this connection. The connection is subtle and unconscious, and it is unfortunately lost very quickly amid the pressures of growing up in the world. Without this access to universal consciousness, or without the Knowledge and Conversation of our Holy Guardian Angels, we humans are blindly groping in the darkness of our conflicted and confused thoughts and feelings.

From the lowest beggar to the richest computer executive, every human being faces insecurity and fear. This is because we have lost the connection with our Holy Guardian Angel, our connection to the universe. As Aleister Crowley put it, "the essence of the horror of not knowing one's Angel is the utter bewilderment and anguish of the mind, complicated by the persecution of the body, and envenomed by the ache of the soul."[2] We can remedy this. Every person can aspire to this knowledge and possess this conversation.

Attaining the Knowledge and Conversation of your Holy Guardian Angel forever transforms your mind, bathing life in the truth and beauty of the universe. This is a magical and spiritual experience that everyone should enjoy. "The illumination and spiritual glory which the Angel brings is so fair and holy and terrible a vision that in the devotee is induced a rapture, an adoration, a transport of ecstasy which is beyond all human conception and human speech,"[3] wrote the noted mystic and initiate Israel Regardie. After such an experience, you are no longer the same.

Once you have attained the Knowledge and Conversation of your Angel, and as long as you heed the counsel of your Angel, your course in life becomes clear. The steps that you must take to achieve your goals are easy, and you can take them confidently. Life becomes a natural and creative expression of your inner beauty. Aleister Crowley wrote, "This is the essential work of every man; none other ranks with it either for personal progress or for power to help one's fellows. This unachieved, man is no more than the unhappiest and blindest of animals . . . . Achieved, he is no less than the co-heir of gods, a Lord of Light. He is conscious of his own consecrated course, and confidently ready to run it."[4]

PART I

Making Space for the Divine

The Knowledge and Conversation of Your Holy Guardian Angel 1

This book is about a spiritual process that has been slowly developing for hundreds of years. This spiritual process is the inner purpose of the entire Western occult movement and is essentially a universal one known by many names: enlightenment, illumination, gnosis, *samadhi*, the oceanic experience, and cosmic awareness, to name a few. In truth, all spiritual paths lead to this same goal. I am exclusively interested in helping you achieve this goal. In this book, the goal is called the Knowledge and Conversation of your Holy Guardian Angel.

"The Knowledge and Conversation of your Holy Guardian Angel" is a rather strange phrase and you may wonder exactly why I insist on using it. Aleister Crowley originally coined the phrase, and no, I don't use it because I'm a big fan of his. I think it is extremely accurate and useful. Crowley defined the phrase in more than one way throughout his voluminous writings, and it's hard to tell exactly what he meant by it. So I'll just tell you what I mean by it.

* Knowledge: Intimate familiarity. In this context, I am using it to mean awareness of the reality of your Holy Guardian Angel.

* Conversation: The ability to communicate.

* Holy: Sacred, worthy of adoration.

* Guardian: Tutelary and protective.

* Angel: Spiritual Being. This being is not some shadowy reflection of your highest ideals; rather, you are a shadowy reflection of this being.

In other words, for me, "The Knowledge and Conversation of your Holy Guardian Angel" means quite simply the awareness of and ability to communicate with your highest spiritual being.

What Is the Holy Guardian Angel?

You may now be thinking that this Angel is just a metaphor, or you may still be holding on to the notion that a golden-winged being of light awaits you in some invisible realm. To tell the truth, directing your energy toward figuring out what an Angel really is will not bring you any closer to the Knowledge and Conversation. Having said that, let me make a few points of clarification.

You might hear the Holy Guardian Angel referred to as the Higher Self. This is not inaccurate, but it can be misleading. The Holy Guardian Angel is not you in any sense of your current concept of you. Many people think of their Higher Self as the best and most spiritual part of their personality. The Higher Self is their generosity, loving-kindness, intuitiveness, and so forth. None of this has anything to do with your Holy Guardian Angel. Your Holy Guardian Angel might encourage you to be generous, or may inspire loving-kindness, but it is not any part of your personality. It would be safe to consider it as a separate being, because it is so foreign that you may be unable to reconcile your Angel with your self, even though your Angel dwells in your own innermost center.

The reason for this is quite simple. You are not the product of your own being. You are currently an amalgam of family and cultural tendencies combined in a unique way, juxtaposed on top of a spiritual infinity. The *real* you is something of which you are, for the most part, unaware, although you may feel some faint cry of longing from this inner being as you wake up each morning to go, once again, to a job that you did not choose for love but rather for convenience, to work on projects that are not your own. This is certainly not to say that quitting your job is the key to spiritual unfolding. Spiritual unfolding takes place as you awaken to the karmic forces that have propelled you to where you are now and discover that you do not even know the real you.

Over the centuries, the Holy Guardian Angel has been called by hundreds of names, including the Logos, the Augoeides, the Genius, the Higher Self, the Inner God, Silent Watcher, Great Master, the Daemon, Adonai, Vishnu, Atman, The Great Person, and even the Qabalistic terms Neschamah, Chiah, or Yechidah. Abramelin the Mage and Aleister Crowley chose the name "Holy Guardian Angel." The name implies no particular theory of the universe, and it would be silly if not impossible to try to erect a cosmology around the name.

Don't confuse the Holy Guardian Angel with any aspects of your personality, for there is no direct relationship between any part of your personality and the Holy Guardian Angel. Your Holy Guardian Angel is not a human construct; it is beyond that. If you hear somebody talking about their Angel as an interdimensional being or that they are communicating with Atlantis through their Angel, they are talking about something other than the Holy Guardian Angel.

I want to share with you a really big secret: you already have the Knowledge and Conversation of your Holy Guardian Angel. You just don't know it. It's really strange, but once you experience this cosmic awareness, you realize that it's always been there. There is so much other stuff going on around you that it distracts you from the *pure ecstacy* of being that you're experiencing *right now*. The silent voice of your Holy Guardian Angel is always with you. It is not somewhere else in some distant, lofty, spiritual sphere. It is deep inside you. If you listen, truly listen, you can hear it beckoning even now. It is a soft voice, and you have to listen carefully. It is easy to mistake this voice for the many other voices inside your head. The way to tell that the voice is your Angel is that it will always be in favor of you, a quiet advocate. It is always encouraging you in and toward love.[1]

These words from Aleister Crowley nicely sum up what the Holy Guardian Angel is: "The Angel is an actual Individual, with his own universe, exactly as man is. . . . He is not a mere abstraction, a selection from, and exaltation of, one's own favourite qualities. . . . He is something more than a man, possibly a being who has already passed through the stage of humanity, and his peculiarly intimate relationship with his client is that of friendship, of community, of brotherhood, or fatherhood."[2]

Thou Shalt Have No False Holy Guardian Angels

There is a very popular "angel movement" going on in Western culture these days. Little "guardian angel" lapel pins, and workshops on "working with your angel guides" abound. One of the main reasons that I have written this book is to throw the floodlight of sanity upon this flim-flam that has been infecting the Western mind.

The main thing that I would like to get across on this subject is that each person has one Holy Guardian Angel, and only one. Many of the self-proclaimed angel experts these days assert that we each have many angel guides and we can work with them all and get just so much more angelic guidance that way. These "angels" certainly exist, and you can definitely work with myriad spirits, disembodied entities, totem animals, and archetypal figures. There is nothing wrong with doing this. In fact, it is quite useful in many ways. But these entities are not "guides." These entities are not yours. Most of them are unbalanced forces that are seeking to reach equilibrium through your perceptual system. Some of these entities exist inside of you and some outside of you. They are unconscious forces that you need in your life, forces that you are probably drawn toward or fascinated by, but you should not consider them your advisors.

Your Holy Guardian Angel is entirely different from these entities in every way. In essence, your Holy Guardian Angel is the center of your universe, the pivot point, the axis on which your consciousness revolves. To propose that there are many of these angels is to propose that we have more than one axis, more than one center of being. It is just not accurate. Your Holy Guardian Angel is the purveyor of your purpose in life, which is also singular. If you do this one thing—your purpose—you are unstoppable. If you try to do some other thing on the advice of some "angel spirit guides," disparate forces may eventually pull you to pieces.

Some people try to suppress all sorts of anger and despair beneath a love-and-light surface, which any psychologist will tell you, is unhealthy. There is a good reason why "New-Agers" are sometimes regarded as "spaced-out." By submitting to the power of unbalanced archetypes, people allow themselves to be vampirized. They ask the advice of the "blue angel" and then the "purple angel" and then the "lavender angel," and each one gives them differing and opposing instruction. They feel like they're becoming truly enlightened. On the contrary, these colorful guides are soaking up all the original and unique life-energy of these individuals.

One exception among the New Age literature is Edwin Steinbrecher's *The Inner Guide Meditation*. This book contains a method of contacting your "Inner Guide," a figure who is, in my experience, a personified symbol of your Holy Guardian Angel on the astral plane. The inner guide meditation is a simple way of contacting your Holy Guardian Angel through the subjective figure of an "Inner Guide." Using this system, you can speak with your inner guide and obtain advice and help on your spiritual path. The method is so lucid and useful that I recommend it highly to anyone looking for a truly easy and flexible technique. The inner guide meditation does have its limits, and may seem overly simplistic to anyone who is really steeped in the Western occult movement.

One of the most important things that I realized by using simple techniques such as Steinbrecher's is that your Holy

Guardian Angel is always with you. You can have your Angel right this moment, if you want. The Angel is there, perched and waiting above and within you. You can speak now, and if you listen, you will hear an answer. Other voices may answer at the same time. Some of these other voices may say that you're being foolish, that there are no angels, and that this book is silly. Your angel's voice will actually be easy to recognize amid the throng. It may be loud, or it may be silent, but in it will be honesty and love. It will be a voice that is, in truth, more *you* than anything you've ever known of yourself. The voice is intimate, familiar, never lofty or full of itself. When you hear this voice, there is no question that it is your Angel. You may not be ready to hear what it has to say, but perhaps you can catch a whisper. I dare you to speak to your Angel right now. Ask. I double-dog dare you. The degree of bliss that you feel in response is the degree to which you are presently capable of communicating with your Holy Guardian Angel.

Many people think that enlightenment, gnosis, or the Knowledge and Conversation of the Holy Guardian Angel come like a cataclysm. They think that if they just keep doing some sort of technique over and over, one day, *someday*, they'll become illumined in some sort of divine thunderstorm. It is true that you will have peak experiences—explosive oceans of bliss that will change you forever—if you follow a serious practice. However, for the most part, spiritual growth is like cultivating a plant or garden. It grows little by little, season by season, until one day you realize that you have a beautiful and illuminated soul. Often this realization is as cataclysmic as any samadhi.

People have constructed many different models of the subtle realms beyond the physical plane. There is the Theosophical model, the Qabalistic model, the Vedantic model, the Taoist model, the neoshamanic other-realm model, and hundreds of others. You must remember that these are simply models. They do not represent truth. Whatever you experience is the truth, and the most that anyone can ever hope to provide you is a very blurry map.

For the purposes of this book, I will outline a very simple model so you have an understanding of the terms I use. Essentially, we can divide the experiential universe into four realms: the physical, the astral, the causal, and the divine. The world that we look at when our eyes are open is the physical realm. The world we look at when our eyes are closed is the astral realm. The source that generates the images in the astral realm is the causal realm, and the source of consciousness itself is the divine realm.

Your Holy Guardian Angel is your personal connection to the most subtle realm—the divine realm. This divine realm is beyond words, thoughts, feelings, or images. It is pure bliss. Any image that you "see" or words that you "hear" from your Angel are not truly the reality of your Angel. They are reflections coming to you and will be somewhat garbled and warped by your ego's whims and desires. This is why you will work toward attaining a complete silence and singular concentration on the essence of your Angel. It is only in this transcendental way that you can really experience the complete truth unedited by illusion.

So, in conclusion, you can work with many spirits, angels, and archetypes, but your Holy Guardian Angel is beyond these—a singular essence. These multiple spirits are not dangerous unless you confuse them for your Holy Guardian Angel. They can even be helpful assistants and bestowers of gifts. You can communicate with your Holy Guardian Angel this moment if you wish. However, it is only in the transcendental silence beyond images, words, and feelings that you can really know the truth of your Angel and your Self.

The Book of the Sacred Magic of Abramelin the Mage

The seed for the spiritual process of the 21st-century mage is a book called *The Book of the Sacred Magic of Abramelin the Mage*, which, for simplicity's sake, I will refer to as *The Abramelin*. Written in the 15th century, the book describes a six-month operation for obtaining communication with your "guardian angel," and thus magical powers over evil spirits. *The Abramelin* was translated into English by S. L. MacGregor Mathers, one of the founders of the 19th-century occult group, The Hermetic Order of the Golden Dawn. Mathers considered it to be a quaint commentary on the task of the "Adeptus Minor," who, as an initiate of The Golden Dawn, was supposed to achieve communion with his or her "Higher Genius." Many legends arose from *The Abramelin* while Mathers was translating it, including stories about accidents and injuries inflicted by its evil spirits upon those who possessed the book. When Aleister Crowley became a member of the Golden Dawn, Mathers was finishing his translation, and the rumors of curses and injuries were at their height. The legends and the lofty style of *The Abramelin* undoubtedly impressed the young and imaginative Aleister Crowley, and he made it a cornerstone of his spiritual world. It is Crowley who really puzzled over the process described in *The Abramelin*, and when he formed his own magical order, the A∴ A∴, the whole purpose of the teachings was to accomplish the Abramelin Work. "The Grade of Adeptus Minor is the main theme of the instructions of A∴ A∴. It is characterized by the Attainment of the Knowledge and Conversation of the Holy Guardian Angel."[3]

Many experts believe *The Abramelin* to be the simplest and most effective explanation of the secret Western spiritual doctrine. Since S. L. Macgregor Mathers translated it at the turn of the 19th century, it has been a staple on the bookshelves of most serious students of the occult.

The author of *The Abramelin* is known only as Abraham the Jew, a wandering scholar who claims to have discovered the true secrets of magic and spirituality from an Egyptian magician named Abramelin, after whom the book is named. Abraham describes his adventures before and after meeting his magical mentor, but primarily focuses on the methods of performing an extended spiritual operation that eventually culminates in the Knowledge and Conversation of the Holy Guardian Angel.

Much of the advice in *The Abramelin* may seem somewhat strange to the modern mind. For instance, the book advises you not to sleep with your wife when she's menstruating (with no advice for you if you happen to be a woman!), that you should change your personal garment once a week (for the purpose of cleanliness!), and many other strange, archaic ideas. This aspect of the book can (and should) be safely ignored. In general, *The Abramelin* requires careful interpretation rather than blind adherence to rules that have little practical meaning in modern life.

Between the time of *The Abramelin* and today, modern adepts have added many improvements upon the basic plan of Abramelin. This book will share with you some of these improvements, so that you may benefit from them as well.

Dispelling the Abramelin Myths

I have heard a number of incredibly silly things about the Abramelin operation. It seems that some otherwise perfectly intelligent students have dreamed up some crazy, strict rules that they believe must be followed in order to pursue this path. Fortunately, none of the following beliefs have anything to do with the Abramelin operation, either as it exists in the book or in its practical performance. I feel that most of the moral and behavioral instructions in *The Abramelin* should be taken with a grain of salt, but I have created the following list of myths to help you separate the silly from the essential.

MYTH NO. 1: YOU MUST LIVE ALONE IN THE WOODS TO PERFORM THE OPERATION.

There is simply no basis for this *anywhere* in *The Abramelin*. The author repeatedly describes your continued relations with your wife and your neighbors, and he gives provisions for performing the operation in the middle of a town. The only place where the woods are even mentioned is in a single phrase that states that the perfect place for your temple would be "where there is a small wood, in the midst of which you shall make a small Altar, and you shall cover the same with a hut of fine branches, so that the rain may not fall thereon and extinguish the Lamps and the Censer."[4] However, this is one statement, and it is talking about the place for your temple, not your living arrangements. Many other statements in the book seem to contradict this idea altogether, implying that the entire operation could even be performed by a servant living in someone else's home. The book admits this would be difficult, but it does not exclude the possibility. The woods are definitely optional.

MYTH NO. 2: YOU MUST ISOLATE YOURSELF FROM THE WORLD.

Again, there is no basis for this. There are numerous instructions for being generous with your neighbors, and giving alms to the poor. Hermits could do neither. You don't have to leave your wife. You don't have to abandon your children.

Myth No. 3: You must devote all of your time to the operation.

Actually, during the first two-thirds of the operation, you devote to it only two hours or less each day. The last part of the operation requires about four hours a day, and your focus should be primarily on the operation throughout the day, but this will be automatic by then. Still, all of this is safely within the time most people spend watching television. I don't think that's too much too ask in exchange for a connection with your divine and creative genius.

Myth No. 4: The operation requires a huge amount of work.

Again, it's a series of some prayers, ceremonies, and/or meditations. There is nothing "huge" involved. The only difficulty that arises is confronting your own personal conflicts and the need to develop discipline. Both of these things are required of any human who hopes to do anything meaningful in life.

Myth No. 5: Only an Adeptus Minor in A∴A∴ can do the operation.

Abraham the Jew mentions nothing whatsoever on this subject. He seemed blissfully unaware of any special rules for adepts. However, Aleister Crowley's "Liber VIII" has something quite clear to say on the subject, "And even if he be of higher rank than a probationer, he shall yet wear the robe of a probationer . . ."[5] In other words, anyone of whatever rank is invited to perform this operation. And this is straight from an Angel's mouth.

Myth No. 6: Only crazy people try this operation.

Well, maybe this myth is true.

The Abramelin Program 2

The operation described in *The Abramelin* takes more or less six months to complete. You shouldn't rush it if it seems to be taking longer, but on the other hand, you might complete it in a shorter amount of time. As Aleister Crowley put it, "The Holy Guardian Angel has always the necessary basis. His manifestation depends solely on the readiness of the Aspirant, and all magical ceremonies used in that invocation are merely intended to prepare that Aspirant; not in any way to attract or influence Him. It is His constant and eternal Will to become one with the Aspirant, and the moment the conditions of the latter make it possible, That Bridal is consummated."[1]

However, it is certainly best to prepare to spend at least six months on the operation. This may seem a long time, but it's really just about the amount of time that passes between Christmas and Memorial Day. It flies by. The work will also be progressive. In the beginning, you will need to do only a small amount of work. It is only toward the end that much effort will be required.

When to Begin the Abramelin Operation

The Abramelin suggests that the best time to begin this operation is around the time of the Easter celebration. The very best time would seem to be on the day of the vernal equinox, at the end of March. Since the operation takes six months, it would then be concluded at the autumnal equinox, at the end of September.

The main reason to start at the vernal equinox is that most spiritual traditions consider this the perfect time for new beginnings. It is the time of the ascension of Christ, the Passover, and Alban Eilir, the festival of spring. It is the season where new growth first starts in the fields, when life is renewed on Earth. However, this holiday-based scenario is unnecessary. If it's really your will to do this operation, you could start today. What the heck!

The Phases of the Operation

The actual six months of the operation comprise three two-month periods. These three periods may take two months each, or they may be shorter. You may find that you naturally move from one phase to the next in any period of time. You will begin the first period by taking an oath to complete the operation (see p. 39). Taking an oath is the most important way to begin. You will be able to make it through the entire operation only by sticking to the letter of your oath. At a certain point, you may weary of the whole thing and experience "the dark night of the soul." You will have a chance of finishing only because you have sworn yourself to complete the operation.

The First Two Months

Throughout the first period, you will need to develop some discipline. The work will be easy, but you must be sure to do it. If you begin to slip up in the beginning, you are sure to crumble before the end. This is true of any spiritual practice. You should enter your temple at least once a day, and perform some sort of prayer or meditation.[2] *The Abramelin* is deliberately vague about the content of this prayer, except that you must confess all of your sins.[3]

In these two months, you should learn to explore yourself and discover what kind of prayer or meditation suits you best. You can feel comfortable experimenting at this stage, and not worry about achieving anything significant. As Abramelin says, "Know ye that although in the beginning your prayer be but feeble, it will suffice, provided that ye understand how to demand the Grace of the Lord with love and a true heart, whence it must be that such a prayer cometh forth."[4] In other words, it is perfectly all right to feel like you're doing everything wrong and badly, as long as your goal is to understand the universe.

At this stage, be sure that you do whatever practice you adopt without fail. *The Abramelin* suggests that you do these practices at dawn and at sunset. However, if necessary, you may practice at whatever time is most convenient, so long as you stick to your schedule. In other words, if you decide to do your practices at 9 A.M., make sure you really do them at that time every day. It's okay to be a little late or early, as long as you don't skip it.

According to Abramelin, you should also devote some time in your life outside of your practices to exploring the world's religious texts. If you feel strongly about a particular religion or philosophy, you can read the scriptures of that faith. If you are interested in no specific religion, it might be a good idea to study comparative religion, philosophy, or even psychology.

Slowly but surely, the correct ways for you to improve the practices that you're doing will spontaneously begin to occur to you. You will discover on your own the most effective ways for you to reach into the cosmos with your whole heart. When this happens, you will know that you are making progress. You will then be ready for the second stage.

The Second Two Months

After two months or so, you will probably have discovered many fascinating things about yourself, but you may also be getting quite tired of your daily practices. If you make it to two months without a single slip, you should congratulate yourself, because many people fail much sooner.

Although you may be getting bored after two months, rather than stop or slow down, you must increase your work. You still need only perform one or two daily practices, but you must truly put your all into them. Make sure that you incorporate some of the improvements you have come up with into your practices at this stage.

In the second stage, it is easiest to start slipping into a simple routine and making a habit out of your practices, so try to put some effort into keeping your practices fresh and real. Make sure that you truly put your all into every single practice, and try to extend the amount of time you spend on each practice. This will become truly difficult after a short time. Once you feel like you can't go on, that your practice is useless and that you are wasting your time, you are finally ready for the third stage.

The Last Two Months

In the last two months, you will need to increase your practice to two or three times a day, and in between, little else should be on your mind. The full force of your being should be propelling you toward your Angel.

At the end of the six months or the natural conclusion of these three stages, whether shorter or longer, you will fervently invoke your Angel with the whole of your heart. If you follow this outline, augmented by the further instruction throughout this book, in six months' time you will truly discover your Angel.

Preparation for the Abramelin Operation 3

The purpose of the Abramelin operation is to make a permanent change in yourself and your relationship with the universe. Because of this, you might want to implement some behavioral changes from the beginning, and I will discuss these in this chapter. Additionally, before undertaking Abramelin's operation, it is important to consider some of the provisions that *The Abramelin* insists upon. Although you may choose to ignore them, it would be irresponsible of me not to point them out to you.

Dedication and Resolve

For centuries, this magick has been handed down from master to pupil, and by receiving it, you have gained something truly "sublime and precious." The best way to make yourself worthy of this special gift is to devote yourself to the task of gaining the Knowledge and Conversation of your Holy Guardian Angel with your whole heart. Devote yourself absolutely to universal awareness. By doing this you will devote yourself to yourself, to your own self-knowledge and self-love. There could be no more worthy task.

You must seriously consider whether you truly intend to carry out the operation to the end. If you are not going to finish, it is better that you don't even begin. It may do irreparable harm to your psychological state to work through half of the program and then give up. On the other hand, if you have a fixed resolve to complete the operation, you will be able to complete it with ease.

Personal Resources

According to Abramelin, you should also be sure that your financial situation is conducive to this serious endeavor. If you do not have sufficient resources available to you, you will not be able to focus enough energy on higher consciousness. Food and rent will always come before spirituality. That's just the way life works in the real world. Abramelin states that you may continue to work at your profession throughout the operation, but I do agree with the implication that competing for promotions or dealing with the stress of monetary needs may hold you back from the necessary focus. On the other hand, you should not let poverty keep you away from your spiritual needs. Gaining the Knowledge and Conversation of your Holy Guardian Angel may be the perfect way to get your life together enough to build financial freedom for yourself. The most important thing is to follow your heart.

Social Commitments

Abramelin advises that you also consider your social situation. If you are married, involved in a serious relationship, or if you have children, you must decide whether the relationship will interfere with or be damaged by this work. I foolishly ignored this advice and experienced much anguish trying to hold my relationships and my spiritual practice together all at the same time. I urge you to consider the ramifications of a daily regimen. Talk it over with your partner. Make sure that your partner understands exactly what you are going to be doing. If you don't, you're just asking for trouble.

It's important to make sure that your partner knows you're not trying to replace him or her and that the operation is not going to take away all of your time together. My girlfriend was extremely jealous of my Holy Guardian Angel for several weeks until we had a heart-to-heart talk about it. I think it's important for both partners to negotiate and communicate their needs. Then you'll have a smooth time of it, except for the inevitable arguments. However, starting from an understanding will save you a lot of time in the end.

Plan to avoid unnecessary complications during the period of your operation. Distractions such as new or complex emotional relationships or new business ventures will tend to hold you back. Of course, we all live in the real world, so you will have unexpected troubles and tribulations. Your troubles may actually be magnified as soon as you begin. I know my personal life became totally insane as soon as I started the operation. Just try to avoid the complications in your life that you *can* avoid. Idle relationships and redundant conversations will keep you stuck in old ways of looking at the world. You need to free yourself from worldly concerns, and get in touch with the center of your being. If you do not attempt to put yourself above the demands of the everyday world, you will remain unchanged.

This does not mean that you have to quit your job and go to the desert in order to succeed. It merely means that you should minimize your distractions. A meditative life is probably necessary, but becoming a hermit is certainly not required. Withdrawing from involvements should help you along in your spiritual development; it's not meant to be a contest of your "spiritual mettle."

Your Health and Safety

Abramelin feels that the most important thing to consider is your health and safety. You must be healthy in both mind and body in order to pursue this work. "A sick man can neither be clean and pure, nor enjoy solitude; and in such case it is better to cease."[1] However, when I started the operation I was twenty pounds overweight, a heavy smoker, and in extremely poor physical condition. During the course of my practice, I had a fever of 104 degrees for several days, and a few serious colds. I did not miss a single day of my practices. Since I began the operation, I have lost 15 pounds, maintained a daily exercise routine, and quit smoking. The Abramelin operation inspired me to correct several health problems and personally destructive behaviors. Perhaps you'll find that even if you're sickly at the start, you may become an entirely new person by the end.

Your Sacred Space

Throughout the six months or so of your practice, you will need to set aside a special, sacred place for the work. Privacy is paramount. You must find a place that is yours alone. If you are doing the operation in your home, dedicate some part of it as your temple. Ideally, you would devote a whole room to the effort. If space restrictions prevent you from devoting an entire room to the operation, an area of some room will suffice. Whether a whole room, or part of a room, the area must be clean and free of clutter. Only objects that specifically relate to your work should be kept in the area. Dirty laundry, photographs, toys, and these sorts of things can only serve to distract you from your purpose.

According to *The Abramelin*, you should consider your bedroom holy throughout the operation. It is to be kept as clean as your temple, for the same reason. If your temple is a small part of your bedroom, then you can easily meet both requisites. *The Abramelin* states that no animals and as few human guests as possible should be allowed in either your bedroom or your temple, for they will apparently dampen the sense of sacredness that your space must accumulate. Again, this is all medieval stuff and can be obeyed or ignored at your discretion.

The Temple

In an ideal situation, you would perform your operation in a place where you can obtain absolute solitude, the very best being, as it says in *The Abramelin*, "where there is a small wood."[2] However, since few of us can find such a situation, we have to make a few adjustments. At the very least, you should have a small space that is absolutely devoted to your work, where you will be undisturbed and where you can feel comfortable performing any rite or practice without the fear of disturbing or being interrupted by neighbors or roommates. If you cannot manage that, do not despair; even a small corner fitted with a nice carpet or cloth could serve as your temple. "With God all things are possible," as the saying goes.

The Altar

Your altar for the Abramelin operation can be anything, such as a small table or cabinet, but you must dedicate it solely to the project, and not use it for other things. The reason for this is quite simple. If you're using it for other things, you will think of those things while you are using your altar. Your altar should make you think of your Angel alone. You will purify it, consecrate it, and, as much as possible, protect it from being touched by anyone but you. Ideally, the altar will be made of wood with a cupboard inside where you can stash all your magical implements. The purpose of the altar is to hold your incense censer as you burn your special incense for your angel each day. It may not seem important to have this altar, but its significance will grow in your mind as you proceed. Don't skip it.

The Oil of Abramelin

According to Aleister Crowley, "The Holy Oil is the Aspiration of the Magician; it is that which consecrates him to the performance of the Great Work; and such is its efficacy that it also consecrates all the furniture of the Temple and the instruments thereof."[3] The oil that you are to use is the "Oil of Abramelin," which is prepared from myrrh, cinnamon, and galangal mixed with olive oil. It is available from several sources already made. I would suggest looking online or checking with your local esoteric or New Age stores. If you decide to make Oil of Abramelin yourself, you should not dump the actual herbs into olive oil; use their essential oils. Its color should be a rich, clear, gold to represent your highest ideals. You can use this oil to consecrate yourself daily if you wish, but you must consecrate yourself with it at the start of the operation, and consecrate any tools that you will use.[4]

The Incense of Abramelin

Many people are confused about the Abramelin incense. They think that it is made from the mixed and ground dry ingredients of the Abramelin oil, which actually results in a foul-smelling mess. True Incense of Abramelin is made of 1 part frankincense, 1/2 part storax, and 1/4 part lign aloes. If you can't find storax and lign aloes (they're expensive and somewhat rare), you can replace storax safely with myrrh, and lign aloes with cedar or sandalwood. Reduce the ingredients to a fine powder and mix them well. Every time you burn this incense, its pretty and delicate fragrance will help exalt your mind.

Your Robes

I highly recommend that you use some special clothing dedicated to the operation, for your robes will come to symbolize your operation, and each time you don them, you will immediately begin to shift into a devotional mindset. According to *The Abramelin*, you will need two tunics—one of linen, and the other of crimson or scarlet silk with gold. You could replace these with any kind of meditation clothing, depending on your technique. For example, if you are focusing on yoga techniques, you may wish to wear loose silk pants. For ritual magic, you might choose a simple black robe.

The Wand

After you have attained the Knowledge and Conversation of your Angel, you will probably need a magick wand.[5] A magick wand is the symbol of your will. It represents the straight line of your aspiration and your ability to direct your force toward your goal. Your wand is therefore a symbol of the power given to you by your Holy Guardian Angel. When you wield your wand, you are directing the forces of your own creation toward manifestation. According to Abramelin, you should cut the wand from an almond tree, but it is really a matter of personal choice. Your wand is your tool, and you should construct one that meets your needs.

The Crown

You may decide that you need a crown or magical cap. This may be made to your liking, but it should express your highest ideals, and assert your authority over the spirit kingdom. A crown is the symbol of the completion of your work, and the highest aspects of the universe.

These items may or may not seem necessary to you because of the way that you choose to approach the operation. They are symbols, and all of them are symbolically necessary. Whether or not you create physical representations of these objects, you *will* be using all of them in the operation. For instance, you may not feel the need for a wand because you have chosen to use yoga techniques and not ceremonial magick. In this case, your wand is nothing less than your own spinal cord. Each of these tools has an inner significance that will become clear as you proceed. The altar represents the physical conditions surrounding your aspiration, while the oil and incense represent the aspiration itself. The robes represent your spiritual body, and the crown represents the divinity that is above and within you. You can use all of these symbols physically, or you can mentally incorporate them into your aspiration.

The Foundation of Your Spiritual Practice 4

The operation in *The Abramelin* is not particularly complex, but it requires a serious commitment of both time and energy. The relationship that will form between you and your Holy Guardian Angel is very powerful and serious. You will be permanently transformed by the time you are done. This is a real and potent undertaking. You must understand this before you begin, because not taking this seriously could result in real catastrophe. As Abramelin puts it, "a few ill-words pronounced by an ill-intentioned person only produce an effect against the person himself who pronounceth them; and an individual of such a character should in no way attempt this Operation, for such would be the true way to make a mock of God and tempt him."[1] If you are not ready for such a serious endeavor, hold off until the time is right.

Having said that, I want you to understand that this is the most wonderful pursuit, and will fill your life with great power and joy. This operation is what the ancients called "The Great Work," the *Magnum Opus*, the key to "True Wisdom and Perfect Happiness."

The wonderful thing about the Abramelin operation is its flexibility. There are several ways to achieve success with this system. The core of the practice is to approach the universe, or God, from your innermost self. As Abramelin says:

> It is absolutely necessary that your prayer should issue from the midst of your heart, because simply setting down prayers in writing, the hearing of them will in no way explain unto you really how to pray. This is the reason that I have not wished to give you any special form of prayers and orations, so that ye yourselves may learn from and of yourselves how to pray, and how to invoke the holy name of God, our Lord.[2]

In the following chapter, I will explain the framework of your practice: retirement, the oath, the confession, purity, consecration, and the Eucharist. I will also outline a number of different approaches to prayer so that you can explore this operation from a number of angles and find the best way to proceed for yourself. Prayer is actually any activity that is intended to connect you spiritually to the universe. This could mean different things to different people: chanting, silent meditation, dancing, or sex. The only limiting factor is your own imagination.

The basic structure of the Abramelin operation is very simple. You will enter your temple daily, burn sacred incense, and perform some sort of spiritual activity (or prayer). The purpose of this activity is to purify your being, and to raise your spirit to higher and higher levels of refinement. What this activity specifically consists of is totally up to you. It is the repetition and the continued fervor with which you pursue the activity that will bring about changes in your spiritual makeup, which will transform you. The activity must have the tendency to draw you up into the inner, spiritual realms, rather than simply being a dull repetition. In Part II, we will explore several different methods of approaching this spiritual awakening.

When you are leading your life outside of your temple, make an effort to continue this purifying process. This is simply a matter of avoiding complicated life situations and generally being a decent, pleasant person to those around you. This will most likely happen without much effort, because your daily spiritual efforts will inspire you in this direction anyway. You will, of course, behave poorly and treat people badly from time to time during the operation, but this is only to be expected. The operation works to clear away the toxicity from your being so that you can access higher consciousness. It is only natural for you to express some of this toxicity as you go along.

The simplicity of the Abramelin operation baffles many, who try to make it more complex than it need be. If you pursue any of the specific methods in this book, or any that you come up with yourself, for the six-month period, with commitment, enthusiasm, and expectation, you will transform. It is that simple.

Retirement

In order for you to transcend your fears and experience the reality of your divine interior, you will need to withdraw from outside influences for an extended period. Even if you do not currently acknowledge that you are constantly in a state of fear, removing yourself from the distractions of ordinary life during the Abramelin operation will enable you to look within yourself and discover your internal life. You don't have to become a hermit. What is required is that you disentangle yourself from other people and focus on yourself. This doesn't mean becoming self-obsessed, it means uncovering the surface layers of your personality to discover what lies inside.

At this moment in time, you are entangled with hundreds of people. Even if you only have a few friends, you still become involved with anybody that you see. As you walk down the street, and someone passes you, you immediately gauge how that person is reacting to you. You decide whether they seem like a nice person. You make sure that they are not going to attack you. All of these things go on under the surface of your consciousness, and you may not even be aware of them.

Take a walk, truly observe yourself, and notice how involved you become in other people. You need to be honest with yourself; it's not going to do you any good to pretend that you are perfect. You will discover that every person you confront has a serious impact on you long after you have left his or her presence. This can be a debilitating situation.

It serves a purpose, of course. If you didn't observe people and categorize them, you could end up being robbed or killed, or miss out on gaining a new friend. The problem is that this categorizing and your emotional, fear-based reaction to the world keeps you tightly closed, and makes connection with your Holy Guardian Angel impossible. These reactions are protective layers that consume most of your energy. You will need to remove these layers in order to make contact with the Holy Guardian Angel.

The easiest way to do that is simply to isolate yourself as much as possible. When you do interact with the world, attempt to remain conscious of your internal reactions.

Having your normal reactions to other people is not harmful as long you are aware that you are having them, acknowledge the reactions, and do not allow them to constrict you.

It is also important for you to avoid becoming involved in other people's problems. Frequently, those that are closest to us depend on us for emotional and psychological support. During the Abramelin operation, you need to concentrate on your emotions and psychology, and becoming entangled in others' problems will only serve to keep you away from your Angel. As Aleister Crowley put it, "A man's friends are more capable of working him harm than strangers; and his greatest danger lies in his own habits."[3] It may be difficult to avoid getting caught up in other people's problems, especially if you are a naturally thoughtful and giving person. Please keep in mind that the help you will be able to give once you are in communication with your Holy Guardian Angel will be so far superior that you will wonder how you could have helped before. Once you have your Holy Guardian Angel, you will no longer be entangled in your own doubts and fears, and you will truly be able to look at the world with clarity for the first time.

The Abramelin insists that you avoid drunkenness, overeating, parties, gambling, and debauchery. It states that you should lead a tranquil life, spending as much time as possible quietly at home, or out enjoying nature. I think this is sound advice.

During the early part of your operation, you will need only to minimize your distractions. You cannot be expected to disappear from the face of the Earth. Simply withdraw yourself slowly, and when you do participate in the world's affairs, remain centered in yourself as much as possible. While you are building toward a feverish conclusion of the operation, however, you will need to isolate yourself almost entirely. Depending on what you do for a living, this may be more or less feasible. At any rate, the important thing is to remain focused on your Angel.

On the other hand, avoiding everything in life can have deleterious effects on your ability to handle the world. Every once in a while, going out and appreciating the world will help you feel "sane." During a period of retirement, you could simply go to a park or the supermarket. You don't need to do anything drastic like going to Mardi Gras or spring break at Daytona Beach. But you should always make sure that you are remaining grounded. You want to improve your relationship with the world, not destroy it.

Enflame Yourself in Praying

"You will begin to enflame yourself in praying, and you will see appear an extraordinary and supernatural Splendour which will fill the whole apartment, and will surround you with an inexpressible odour, and this alone will console you and comfort your heart so that you shall call for ever happy the Day of the Lord."[4]

If you sincerely believe in the sort of God who has a big white beard and sits on puffy clouds, then the Abramelin operation requires little elucidation beyond what is written in the original book. However, such a belief requires a tremendous faith in a nearly animistic God, and the operation will depend on your ability to pray with sincerity for his divine grace and mercy.

We live in an era when most of the people who claim membership in one religion or another live without a real connection to any kind of deity. For many people, prayer has become an empty gesture, and the hope of actually getting anything out of it seems absurd. As J. F. C. Fuller stated almost one hundred years ago, "In these present times prayer has become a mockery, and it is hard, how hard we know well, for any one to pray with that earnestness which brings with it reward. The rationalist has so befouled prayer with his wordy slush that it is indeed a hard task to dissociate it from the host of external symbols and images."[5]

Abramelin presents a perfect, beautiful, and simple method of attaining the Knowledge and Conversation of your Holy Guardian Angel, of establishing that universal, transcendental awareness, but for most people the method would seem hardly to have a chance of working. We need to take a look at the nature of prayer, and specifically into the kind of prayer that Abramelin prescribes. In truth, the only specific injunction that Abramelin gives as to the method of prayer is that you should "enflame yourself in praying."

What you are trying to do is to make a connection and establish a relationship with the greater consciousness of the universe. Your normal consciousness is unable to make such a connection, so it is necessary to "enflame" yourself to the point where you are no longer in your normal state of consciousness.

The purpose of all prayer, meditation, invocation, and mental gymnastics is to direct your consciousness through concentration to a one-pointedness, and in this one-pointedness is the rapture and ecstasy of the vision or conversation with the Holy Guardian Angel. The Christian mystic Miguel de Molinos says on this subject, "O how few are the Souls that attain to this perfect way of praying, because they do not penetrate enough into this internal recollection, and mystical silence . . ."[6]

The true secret lies in the meaning of the word "silence." All of the practices that you will try and learn have the potential of leading you to this internal silence, and the one that works for you is the one you should use. To quote Aleister Crowley, "It is practically of no importance whatever that the invocation should be 'right.' There are a thousand different ways of compassing the end proposed, so far as external things are concerned."7 When you have truly achieved this, the work will be done, and you will have attained the Knowledge and Conversation of your Holy Guardian Angel. What you will discover in this silence is your true nature and the true nature of the universe.

In Eastern metaphysical philosophies it is believed that the human body contains a central pathway through which all of the vital energy that we have at our disposal passes and circulates. It is a hollow channel running up the spine and has been given many names throughout the ages. In Indian yoga philosophy, this channel is known as the *sushumna*. It has also been called the inner reed, inner flute, the path of kundalini, the middle pillar, among other names. As we "enflame" ourselves, whether in prayer, meditation, or sexual devotion, what we are doing is consciously or unconsciously directing energy through this subtle energy channel. When we fully open the channel, the kundalini Shakti rises up to unite with the cosmic Shiva lingam in the brow.8 We could also say that our animal soul rises to unite with our angel, or that Hadit rises to meet Nuit.9 In one way or another, this channel is the pathway that you will travel to discover your Angel, and it is through this pathway that your Angel will become known to you.

You will no doubt discover this inner path or channel on your own, because all of the spiritual development methods—from devout prayer to rising on the planes—make use of it. Crowley's own Holy Guardian Angel said, "But to love me is better than all things: if under the night-stars in the desert thou presently burnest mine incense before me, invoking me with a pure heart, and the Serpent flame therein, thou shalt come a little to lie in my bosom."[10]

Always remember your goal: the Knowledge and Conversation of your Holy Guardian Angel. Anything that you use or do that helps you accomplish that end is what you should do and is the proper way for you to pray.

The Oath

Any change in our lives requires some sort of oath. We swear that although we have been doing something one way for a long time, now we're going to change. Each year, on January 1, many of us make resolutions: we're going to stop eating sweets, we're going to lose some weight, or we're going to stop yelling at our kids. The problem is that most of us don't follow through on these promises. The reason why we don't keep these oaths is that there is an internal "back door" built into most of them. You want to quit smoking, but in the back of your mind you tell yourself things like, "You can't succeed the first time you try," or "Quitting smoking will make it impossible for me to deal with my work load." With New Year's resolutions most people say, "Well, no one really keeps their New Year's resolutions." With these kinds of escape clauses, you are bound to fail.

To begin the operation—or any endeavor toward a goal—without taking an oath to complete it is like saying that you do not intend to complete it. It is giving yourself a wide-open back door. You are virtually saying, "Well, I guess I'll give this a try for a little while, but I'm not guaranteeing that I won't give up in a couple of days." This operation is a serious undertaking, and your success depends on your perseverance.

So, before beginning the operation you must take an oath that you will complete it, and this oath must be unambiguous and inescapable. You cannot overestimate the importance of this step. It is the foundation upon which any work begins. This oath must be a real affirmation of your Will. It is a statement made to the whole universe that you will accomplish the operation.

You can put this oath in writing, but also prepare to say it aloud in your temple. The oath must contain your name, who you are, and why you are addressing the universe. You must state the purpose of your operation—to gain the Knowledge and Conversation of your Holy Guardian Angel. You must state why you are performing this operation. You may have to do some introspection to discover this reason in yourself. And then, you must solemnly swear that you will perform the operation to the end, that nothing will prevent you from completing it. The oath should also contain the manner in which you will perform the operation, for instance, the times you will dedicate to practice, and the amount of time you are dedicating to the operation.

Your oath should also contain information about what experience will constitute success. If you're vague about this, you'll give yourself an easy opportunity to quit. After a couple of weeks you'll feel a little dizzy during one of your practices and you'll say, "Aha! There it is. Enlightenment. I didn't realize how easy that would be." Try to be specific in your description of what this peak experience would have to be like in order for you to be satisfied; for instance, "the oceanic experience of pure consciousness with a silent mind," or, "a vision as real as normal sight of an angelic being who'll tell me my true purpose in life." Neither of these descriptions is an accurate portrait of my own experience, and I do not know what your expectations might be, but these are examples. Your actual experiences may not match those you describe in your oath, but you need to put your expectations in your oath so you won't quit after less than your expected experience. You are making this oath to the universe, and if you make it with sincerity, the universe will always be ready to assist you along your path.

The night before you are ready to begin the Abramelin operation, you need to take formally the oath you have written. You can go into whatever space you are using as a temple and stand in front of your altar, like a soldier preparing to go into battle. You can knock once on the surface of your altar with your fist, as if calling the attention of the universe. In fact, in one way or another, that is exactly what you are doing. Then recite your oath aloud.

Sincerity is a prerequisite, but don't be afraid if you feel a little awkward saying your oath in an empty temple. You are just beginning. People feel most awkward when they are being most genuine. So don't fear awkwardness, it could very well be the real you peeking through for a second. Remember, you are taking an oath. This is no less serious than an oath to your friend or your family or your country. It is much more serious, because it is an oath to the entire universe.

The Confession

"Ye shall enter into your Oratory . . . and place yourselves upon your knees before the Altar. . . . And devoutly and with boldness ye shall invoke the Name of the Lord, thanking him for all the grace which He hath given and granted unto you from your infancy until now; then with humility shall ye humble yourselves unto Him, and confess unto Him entirely all your sins; supplicating Him to be willing to pardon you and remit them."[11]

This is the first instruction *The Abramelin* gives for the operation. On the surface, it seems a quaint, religious archaism. However, it is actually an easy method that can be quite helpful in the operation. This may be especially true if you are compelled by circumstance to maintain a fairly busy schedule while doing the operation. By "confessing" your "sins," what you are really doing is releasing the psychic stress of having those things on your mind. That is the purpose of confession, both religious and magical. It enables you to withdraw from the importance of those things in your life. At least during the time that you are in your temple, you can let the things that are going on in your life go, by "confessing" them to the universe. In Scientific Remote Viewing, a viewer must write down their current Physical and Emotional Distractions, or PEDs, in order to let them go for the time of the operation.[12] This is in essence a modern form of confession. By letting your emotions and thoughts come up to the surface level of your consciousness, you are acknowledging them, and your subconscious is less likely to bring those things up to your conscious mind in the middle of your working.

There is a related, but even deeper, fundamental purpose to confession. If you extend your confession over a period of days or weeks, and repeatedly release all of the emotions, pains, and triumphs that you can recall over the entire span of your life, you will be able to free yourself of an incredibly huge amount of baggage. In essence, you can confess your whole life to the universe, give back all that you have been and done, and then start a new relationship with the universe.

As Miguel de Molinos writes, "The preparation for exterior Souls is to be confessed and retire from the creatures."[13] In other words, the way to universal consciousness is through relinquishing your attachment to the events of your exterior life, and retiring into an interior life.

One of the keys to universal awareness is the ability to be in touch with your original self. "Verily I say unto you, Whosoever shall not receive the kingdom of God as a little child, he shall not enter therein."[14] Children are often thought of as spiritual exemplars because of their joyful innocence and lack of world-weariness. You can easily reclaim this joyful state. All you have to do is think back through the events of your life, let them go, and release your attachment to them. You can free yourself of their hold on you and go back to your original state. According to Miguel de Molinos, "By this way must you return to the happy state of Innocence forfeited by our first parents. By this gate you must enter into the happy land of the living, where you will find the greatest good, the breadth of charity, the beauty of righteousness, the straight line of equity and justice, and, in sum every jot and tittle of perfection."[15]

The burdens of everyday living have hardened you; they have filled you with pain, doubt, and a million other useless things. At this point, it is impossible to view the world without the burden of your preconceived notions. Everything that you see is an echo of some past thing that you saw, and you only see things in reference to those past events. The world you see is essentially a description. You have described the world to your-self, and you spend all of your time maintaining that descrip-tion. If you devote yourself to releasing your experiences back to the universe, you will discover that the world is not at all what you expect. You will be well on your way to discovering your Holy Guardian Angel.

This single technique could be the main focus of your practice, at least for the first few weeks. For many people, this releasing technique would be much more fruitful than trying to silence a turbulent mind. Truly release all of your feelings toward the things you recollect. Simply dwelling on them will get you nowhere.

Making the Confession

The way to begin this practice is to sit or kneel in your temple. Choose a position that will not distract you from the exercise. You may want to bring some pillows into your temple in order to maximize your comfort. Then, you need to relax thoroughly until you achieve a passive state of mind. This is very important.

Next, step-by-step, proceed to recollect the incidents of your life, from the day you begin, all the way back to your earliest childhood memories. This will certainly take more than one day. As the incidents cross your mind, you should acknowledge them, and then release them back to the universe.

The easiest way to do this is to combine your recollecting with breathing. Your breathing should be deep, your diaphragm completely filling and emptying your lungs with each breath (see chapter 7 on yoga techniques for tips on proper breathing and relaxation). Allow any feeling that you need to dislodge come up and discharge with your breathing. Don't be afraid of your feelings—they are just memories and cannot bite you. As you breathe in, pull back all of the energy you have invested in the events you recall, and as you breathe out, give all of that energy back to the universe.

Attempt to recall all of the events of your life in as vivid detail as you can so that you do not secretly hold any things secretly inside. A good way of starting the exercise is to write down all of the major events of your life. You should write down your failures and your victories, your sins and your saintly deeds. Return all of this to the universe. You are not giving up your life, or giving away these things; you are releasing your attachment to them. You are returning to a state of innocence, but innocence with experience.

You may try this exercise before you even begin the Abramelin program, and after a few tries, it will certainly prove valuable, filling you with peace and power. It may even give you the courage to go through with the Abramelin operation. Feel free to try it right now.

Purity and Purification

The Abramelin repeatedly emphasizes purity. According to *The Abramelin,* you must keep your temple, your bedroom, and your body pure. "Your whole attention must be given to purity in all things; because the Lord hath in abomination all that is impure."[16]

Purity is quite important to the operation, but we need to look at the matter of purity from a modern context. It does not necessarily mean that you must scrub the walls of your temple day and night, or that you should wash yourself twenty-five times a day. Purity means singularity. Water that has anything in it aside from water is not pure. Personal purity means directing your energy into one thing and not several. That is why you shouldn't use your temple and altar for other things and why you need to retire from other interests during the period of the operation. Only by focusing on your goal and not allowing other things to interfere can your purpose and intent remain pure. Miguel de Molinos writes, "God has no regard to the multitude of words, but to the purity of intent."[17] It does not matter whether everything that you do is perfect or right, so long as your intention is in accord with your goal.

For the most part, you can easily discard the external instructions for purification as long as you perform your internal purification in a truly dedicated way. For instance, *The Abramelin* suggests that you bathe every Sabbath, and change your garment once a week. In modern times, most of us bathe nearly every day, and we certainly change our garments that often. However, this everyday bathing means little to us.[18]

Daily bathing can easily become a part of your operation, simply by consciously acknowledging it as such. Each day when you bathe, say something to the effect of, "I wash myself so that I may purify myself, so that I may accomplish the Great Work and attain unto the Knowledge and Conversation of my Holy Guardian Angel." This simple dedication then turns your bathing into a sacred act.

Similarly, when putting on your meditation clothes, or any clothes for that matter, you can say, "I now cover myself in these clothes so that I may accomplish the Great Work and may attain unto the Knowledge and Conversation of my Holy Guardian Angel." You may feel silly at first, saying things such as this aloud, but conviction will come with time. You will realize the worth of this practice if you even half-heartedly invest yourself in the endeavor.

When sitting down to eat a meal, you can say, "It is my will to eat and drink, that my body may be fortified, so that I may accomplish the Great Work and may attain unto the Knowledge and Conversation of my Holy Guardian Angel."[19]

By verbally acknowledging each of your acts as a part of your operation, you are taking every opportunity to direct all your consciousness and everything you do toward your purpose. This is the true meaning of purity. You are drawing the force of your mind into your acts, and this fills them with a singular power that is beyond your consciousness. You should make sure that your every act is directed toward the one goal of your Holy Guardian Angel. If you do this with great purity, it won't be long before you achieve your goal.

Additionally, when you begin the Abramelin operation, clean with fresh, pure water all of the things that you are planning to use, such as your robes, altar, pillows, and incense burners, while making a statement such as those in the examples I provided for bathing and eating. By doing this, you are cleansing away any old uses or connections you may have had for these things, and you're freeing them to be dedicated toward the Great Work.

Consecration

Consecration is the next step after purification. It is the active process of dedicating yourself and any object you may want to use toward the goal you have in mind. You purify things to remove all but the single purpose that you intend them for, and you consecrate them to fill them with that single purpose.

Traditionally, purification is performed with water, and consecration with fire. The fire of the consecration is symbolized by either incense or holy oil. Ingredients for both of these things are in chapter 3. The process of consecration is just as easy as purification. Simply take the holy oil and draw upon the object an appropriate symbol (or pass the object through a plume of incense smoke). The equal-armed cross is the most frequently used symbol because it represents the equilibration of the four elements (see chapter 5 for more about the four elements). However, as you draw whatever symbol you choose on whatever you are consecrating, you must dedicate it aloud and in your heart and mind to the purpose for which you intend it.

For example, when you first begin the operation, you would consecrate yourself by anointing your forehead with your holy oil and saying something like, "I consecrate myself in the name of the great singular power of the universe, unto this the Great Work, that I may attain unto the Knowledge and Conversation of my Holy Guardian Angel."

Any object that is a part of your operation should be consecrated in a similar manner, and once it is consecrated, you should never use it for anything else. Once an object is consecrated, keep it wrapped in silk or any other natural fiber, and uncover it only when you use it in your temple. Perform all of your consecrations with as much love and energy as you can summon, because it is this love that will give them their sacred power.

The Eucharist

A Eucharist is performed by taking some object, turning it into something divine, and then consuming it. There are many different kinds of Eucharist. The traditional Roman Catholic Mass contains only one type. There are, in truth, as many different kinds of Eucharist as there are objects and divine things. Anything can be made into a Eucharist, and the highest authorities on spiritual illumination believe that communion of this sort should be undertaken as often as possible. Miguel de Molinos puts it quite plainly, "Frequent communion is an effectual means of getting all virtues, and in particular, internal peace."[20] Aleister Crowley is even more enthusiastic, "A Eucharist of some sort should most assuredly be consummated daily by every Magician, and he should regard it as the main sustenance of his magical life. . . . To a Magician thus renewed the attainment of the Knowledge and Conversation of the Holy Guardian Angel becomes an inevitable task; every force of his nature, unhindered, tends to that aim and goal of whose nature neither man nor god may speak, for that it is infinitely beyond speech or thought or ecstasy or silence."[21]

Anything can become a Eucharist, as long as you dedicate it to that end. By using the power of vocalizing a simple magick spell, you can turn your daily meals into a Eucharist.

Verbally purify and consecrate your food just as previously described. Put the whole force of your being into turning that object into something pure and holy, verbalizing that it is now a holy object, and then consume it solemnly, with the knowledge that you are bringing universal holiness into your body.

Communion need not be restricted to food. You could have communions with sunlight or moonlight. You can turn sexuality into a communion. Nothing should be forbidden from your repertoire. To the pure, all things are pure.

Work on Yourself 5

It is certainly not necessary to be "religious" in any regular sense of the word in order to accomplish the Abramelin operation. In fact, religion is a serious hindrance in this day and age, for doctrines tend to restrict people's thinking. Your Angel is a source of freedom, and therefore cannot be contained within or understood by applying the tenets of most modern religious philosophies. A natural, positive feeling toward God or the universe or whatever you care to call it is an advantage. The important thing is to develop an openness toward the universe. A yearning for understanding and transcendental knowledge is the only prerequisite. All humans have this yearning. Drug abuse, sexual compulsion, overeating, fanaticism in all its permutations—these are all misplaced yearnings for God. The most important thing you can do is simply to *decide* to attain the Knowledge and Conversation of your Holy Guardian Angel. The rest will come on its own.

In this chapter, I provide some information to help you deal with the inner changes you may experience while conducting the Abramelin operation. This information includes my own interpretations of helpful ways of dealing with reality, which I received through communion with my Holy Guardian Angel.

The Four Elements

The ancient Greek philosophers saw the world in terms of four elements: fire, water, air, and earth. The discovery of the four elements is generally credited to the philosopher Empedocles. The word that Empedocles originally used to describe these elements was *rhizai*, meaning "roots." The four elements were, in other words, the source of fire, water, air, and earth. These elements were not the literal things themselves, but poetic expressions of their ideal qualities. Nearly everything could be classified by its nature as related to these four elements. The human mind was no exception. The earth element was seen as the animal needs of the human mind, the water element as the emotions, the air element as the intellect, and the fire element as will.[1]

I see these elements as being the true key to the whole Angelic operation. The Hermetic Order of the Golden Dawn painstakingly initiated a candidate into the four elements as a preliminary to adepthood. While a formal ceremony may not be necessary, a thorough understanding of the elements and how they play out in your personality will prove invaluable. It is by balancing the elements within yourself that you gain a perception of the fifth element, spirit, which binds them all together and balances them into a universal harmony.

Each of these elements corresponds to a distinct way in which a person can look at the world. The first way of looking at the world relates to the earth element. We will call it *perceiving*. Those things that you perceive are seen with the eyes and other physical sense organs. This information seems the most reliable you can get, because it seems to come automatically. This is why it's so insidious. It is by far the least reliable source of information, because it is usually a tool that your ego or your anxieties use to convince you that you see something entirely different. For instance, if you see a dog, and are frightened of dogs, that dog will seem to be a menace no matter how pleasant the dog actually is.

It is also a natural part of our neurology to edit out huge parts of our experience. We tend to see only those things that correspond to our present needs. What's more, we tend to classify things instantly without looking at them individually. When we see a Granny Smith apple, we tend simply to note that it is a "Granny Smith apple," and we miss seeing the apple as it really is. We have a preformed projection of what Granny Smith apples are like, and we only see that projection, unless there is something really distinctive about the particular apple. This is why we often misread titles on books, videotapes or the like when we glance at them only for a second. Our minds are putting up a projection based on experience or some desire to communicate something unconscious to us. Perceiving is, for the most part, our own opinions being projected outward rather than acquiring much new input at all.

The second way of looking at the world is called *understanding* and is related to the water element. Understanding is based upon your emotions. This way of looking at the world is flawed because it is strongly tied to your feelings about yourself, but it is often used to make judgments about others. In other words, you imagine how you would react in another person's place and believe this is the way that person is actually reacting. This is also a projection, and it causes a multitude of problems. Your emotions are the result of experiences over the span of your entire life, and some aspect of them may have developed in very unconstructive ways. For instance, an adult who was physically abused as a child by someone they loved might wince in anxiety when another person touches them lovingly. Your understanding is often manipulated by your own fears, which ultimately injure or enslave you.

Thinking is the third way of looking at the world, and it relates to the air element. This is really the ego's home. The ego only manifests in thoughts. In silence, there is no ego. We might say that the ego is really those thoughts to which we have currently attached importance. Thinking is meant to be a tool and a guardian for us. It is the way that we put the world into a coherent system of experiences. Unfortunately, many of us are slaves to our thought processes. We allow ourselves to think some thoughts, while we disallow others. One of the problems is that we often believe we are thinking when we are really reacting to something that is coming from one of the other modes of looking at the world.

The fourth way of looking at the world is called *knowing,* and it is related to the fire element. The things that you know are all those facts that are simply *so.* You don't have to think about them. They are just fact. Two plus two is four. Water is wet. God is good. Dogs bark. The problem with this way of looking at the world is that it is almost always mixed up with moral concepts. When you know that something is "true" it necessitates the idea that something else is "false." This mode forces you to perceive things in terms of values, and these values are, for the most part, relative rather than absolute. This creates the mass of confusion upon which all moral philosophies are constructed. Good and evil enter in from this mode of looking at the world, and often what seems like a fact is really a judgment, which has nothing to do with fact and everything to do with fears, anxieties, and social taboos.

These four modes of looking at the world interact with each other to create the mild panic in which most people reside. Each of these modes of looking at the world and their related element also correspond to a specific kind of fear. The fears related to the ancient element of earth and physical perception are anxieties about money, health, and anything that has to do with the body or the physical well-being. Often the sufferer will feel all sorts of bodily ills, such as aching bones, headaches, or general weariness. The fears related to water and understanding are those about what others think of you, fears about love and friendship, and feelings of loneliness. Those of air and thinking include fears that you are not intelligent enough, that your decisions are incorrect, or that you are insane. They often manifest as an inability to draw conclusions, or being stuck in overthinking things. Fears related to the ancient element of fire and knowledge are often religious or philosophical, but can include anything to do with guilt, a sense that you are doing something morally wrong, or that somebody else might be doing something wrong.

Luckily, the ancients also perceived a fifth element, which they called "spirit." This element ruled over the others, and kept them in order. It is through this element of spirit that you come into the Knowledge and Conversation of Your Holy Guardian Angel.

There is also a fifth way of looking at the world. It is called *illumination.* It is only through illumination that we truly can have direct experience of the universe, and we can only accomplish this in the silence produced by the spirit element. It is the true way of apprehending reality, because when we have gained control over our elemental personality, we can see beyond our own fears and anxiety. This mode is available to all, but, alas, availed by few.

In Robert Anton Wilson's highly illuminating book *Prometheus Rising,* he compares the four ancient elements to the first four circuits of Timothy Leary's eight-circuit model of consciousness. The first four circuits comprise Circuit I, Bio-Survival, which is the body's program to seek out those things that are pleasant and avoid those that are unpleasant; this relates to Earth, the primitive animal needs. Circuit II is the Emotional-Territorial circuit and rules pack hierarchy, our status in the tribe. It relates to Water. Circuit III is the Time-binding Semantic circuit. It is the first exclusively human circuit, and describes the human need to describe things in words, and with thought. It is related to Air. Circuit IV is the Socio-sexual circuit. It rules the moral life of humans, and is related to the element of fire. As you can see, these circuits correspond fairly exactly with the previous descriptions. Beyond these four circuits, there is a fifth, called the Holistic Neurosomatic Circuit.

In describing the effects of this circuit on the anxieties of the other elements or circuits, Wilson writes, "Fifth Circuit neurosomatic consciousness bleaches out all these problems at once."[2] The complete and total Fifth Circuit experience is none other than the beginning of your connection with the Holy Guardian Angel. In other words, by contacting this Angel, all of your life problems will be "bleached out" by the blissful ecstasy of the experience.

I believe that the four elements and the psychological handicaps that they create are the real secret behind the "four princes" described in *The Abramelin.* These four princes are nothing less than the medieval devils Satan, Lucifer, Belial, and Leviathan. Each of these princes corresponds with one of the ancient *rhizai,* or root elements, and is the personification of the fear that these elements represent. We will discuss these princes more fully in chapter 17.

Each of the four ancient elements has a positive psychological potential as well. The earth element can allow mechanical dexterity, and the enjoyment of physical affection. Water can provide intuition. Air can provide logic and problem-solving skills. Fire can produce the ability to make decisions, and carry through with them. Even if you already experience these things in some degree or another, they are somewhat repressed by self-doubt and anxiety. Once you have attained the Knowledge and Conversation of your Holy Guardian Angel, you will have the ability to be the master of all of these elements, and that will be the beginning of true magical ability.

The Ego

Your ego is essentially a personal conglomeration of all of the forms of fear and perception discussed in the previous section about the four elements. All of the things that seem very important to you—your likes, dislikes, anxieties, religious beliefs—are really just various forms of fear that are not reality-based. You did not choose these fears, beliefs, and values either, although you may not be ready to face this yet. Your whole personality was put together by your parents, environment, and friends as you grew up. Your part in creating it was probably minimal and reactionary. My apologies go to anyone who grew up alone on a desert island—this does not apply to you. For everyone else, the world as you see it is not what it seems. You only see the projections and beliefs that you have been taught to experience.

Every one of us lives inside a bubble. This bubble has been there almost since birth. You live inside it, and what you witness on its round walls is the reflection of your own thoughts and fears. It may seem to be a world that you are seeing, but it is only your world. All you can see is a description of the world as you describe it and as others have taught you to describe it. Outside the bubble is truth, and only when the bubble is burst open can you see the totality of the universe.

Your fears are nothing more than the imaginary wall of this bubble that you have built between you and the universe. It is a wall that you created, and it makes you believe that you are separate from the universe. It is made of all the things that you have done that you do not want the universe to know about, all the secret things that you decided were wrong or too embarrassing to share. This amounts to your entire life. All of this is fear.

The wall of your bubble is your ego. And truly, your ego is simply fear. Once you have released this fear, you will realize that there is no separation between you and the universe and that you are a perfect piece in the puzzle of creation. Before you make a single step on the path toward enlightenment, you must check your ego.

The ego is highly unstable, and if you do not have a conscious connection with your Holy Guardian Angel, the ego tends to rule in its stead. The ego is vulnerable to flattery, attack, ridicule, envy. The Holy Guardian Angel or Higher Divine Self has none of this weakness.

The more you pursue your spiritual practices, the more your ego will complain, object, invoke laziness, and generally attempt to swerve you away from your course. Your ego may also fool you into believing it is your Holy Guardian Angel, which can bring on delusion (or at least get you branded as insufferably righteous). This is because the ego's kingdom will disappear when you realize your connection with the Holy Guardian Angel.

The oath you swear at the beginning of the operation is the key to overcoming this problem. The oath is a catch-22 for the ego. Breaking an oath will damage the ego, so it will attempt to keep it, although perhaps only in letter. It certainly won't want to destroy itself. However, if your oath is iron-clad, containing no loopholes, you can be sure that the ego will eventually crumble.

You may have noticed that I treat the ego as a separate being, almost like a parasite. If you look carefully at the situation, you will discover that your ego is not you at all. The truth is that your ego is just a set of cultural conditions to which you have grown accustomed. It is really nothing at all. When you become upset and defensive about someone offending you, you are defending nothing. The part of you that is worth defending is totally beyond attack. The reality of you is so much more than the mass of superstitions and beliefs by which most people define themselves.

The first step toward breaking through the ego wall is to realize that you are unqualified to judge the conditions of the universe. The question, "Why do bad things happen to good people?" is a fruitless inquiry. No human is singularly qualified to judge what a bad thing is, or who a good person is. It is arrogant to think otherwise. Things merely are, and to judge them on moral grounds is the first mistake of the so-called "righteous person"; this kind of thinking is the worst possible way to use your energy.

When you see someone behaving badly, something that upsets you, someone that you hate, or something that drives you crazy, you must realize that all of these things bother you and deplete your energy only because of the way you have decided to label them. None of these things really means anything. Your enemy is only your enemy because you have made him or her so. The petty, evil acts of others seem petty and evil because your mind allows the concepts of pettiness and evil to hold it prisoner. In reality, the actions of others are merely actions. The causes and effects (the goodness or evilness) of those actions are beyond your conscious ability to know. The correctness or incorrectness of others' actions or behaviors (including the whole universe) can only be a poorly constructed judgment on your part. Fretting and moaning about others is a waste of the little time that you have on Earth. You will not change them—you can only change yourself. By changing, you may even discover that what once seemed an incomprehensible act of evil is actually a necessary and essential part of the universal plan.

When you become dispassionate toward the world, forgetting those things you perceive to be evil, the evils and enemies of your life disappear like the phantoms that they are. What's more, you are rejuvenated. No longer wasting your energy on illusionary grievances, anger, and hatred, a new world of beauty and power opens up before you.

You are responsible for your actions, and no others, and concerning yourself with another person's life makes you subject to the advances of a million useless demons and phantasms of hatred and delusion.

You are a force of nature, a self-luminous star as bright and potent as the Sun, but only when you move as effortlessly as the Sun can you know your own wonder. Then, every step will be in perfect joy, and every path will lead to perfect happiness.

Taking Personal Responsibility for Ourselves

Most of us spend the bulk of our time feeling crappy about one thing or another. We find ourselves in disagreements with others, feeling indignant, wounded, or angry. We feel that our lot in life is quite different from the path that we would like to be on. We don't make enough money, we don't have as many things as we'd like, we don't get the love that we need and deserve. All this comes into play every time we find ourselves at odds with others, and we feel righteous about our own anger. However, very rarely do we take the time to really think about any of these feelings, contenting ourselves with the miserable state we're in by denying that there are any other choices in life.

The simple fact of the matter is that everything in our lives—including all the crappy things—is a choice that we have made for ourselves. That is a difficult fact to face for most of us, since it's much easier to blame random circumstances in our lives than to accept responsibility for our own actions. The first step toward inner and outer peace is accepting responsibility for our lives.

Take, for example a banker who often gets angry because he had always dreamed of being a country-western singer, but in the course of his life, he never bothered to get on a country-western stage at all. Still, he blames his parents, for discouraging him and for sending him to business school, and the country-western music community for never noticing his talent. He blames society for "making" everything so expensive that pursuing your dreams is nearly impossible from a financial standpoint. He blames his wife, for getting pregnant when they were only 21. However, the banker is the one who decided not to pursue his dreams, and any blame must end there.

Taking responsibility for our lives is not just a matter of our work situations. We must take responsibility for everything in our lives—from the greatest to the smallest detail. No one and no thing is capable of effecting any change in us that we do not allow them to make.

If someone tells you that you have a big nose or a flabby stomach, you may feel hurt. However, you must recognize that this injury is one that you are inflicting upon yourself. Even if someone is intentionally trying to hurt you, you are still the only one capable of causing the injury. It is your feelings of inadequacy that come into play. If someone told you that you had a big nose, and you liked your nose, the comment would have little effect. So, in essence, the only injuries that can be inflicted upon you are those that you allow.

"Every man and every woman is a star,"[3] a unique individual, self sufficient and perfect in their own way. Holding ourselves to any standard but our own is both injurious and impractical. We are each perfect in our own way.

This perfection is not subject to comparative analysis, but merely a fact of manifestation. All structures in the universe are in balance, moving harmoniously from unmanifest to manifest and back, in a cyclical motion. This state of balance and invulnerability is the natural state for all human beings. Invoke it, and you can live it.

To make the statement that there is something wrong with you is to claim that the universe made some sort of error in your creation. Your perfection is unknown to you as long as you deny it.

If you insist upon injuring yourself with your perceived inadequacies, you will not be able to fulfill your own perfection. The way to the Knowledge and Conversation of your Holy Guardian Angel is forgiveness of yourself.

The next time you find yourself in conflict with someone, instead of placing blame upon the other person, look at yourself in the situation. Look at yourself and remember that there are no wrong feelings. Forgive yourself in advance for whatever you may find. Notice how you are feeling. At first, you probably won't even know how you are feeling, or you may think it is anger. In a few moments, if you look deeply within, you will find that what you really feel is fear.

You probably won't even know what you are afraid of, but when something in life upsets you, it is a manifestation of your fear. It is just one of those four elemental forms of fear, creeping into your consciousness. Anger is a form of fear. Sadness is a form of fear. Loneliness is a form of fear. Still, even recognizing this, it is not easy to let go of that fear. You feel afraid right now. If you didn't, you would be experiencing the Knowledge and Conversation of your Holy Guardian Angel. You have covered the true experience of your Angel with the illusion of fear. You were taught fear, and you have been fearful for so long that any other condition seems almost impossible.

Avoiding Habits

In your day-to-day life, you spend nearly all of the energy at your disposal on a set of routines. These routines are so implanted that you consider them to be you. They are more than the way you drive to work each day or the brand of soap you buy—they are the way that you fundamentally interact with your environment. Everything that you think about, every aspect of your life is just a routine, a conditioned response. For the most part, you live in the past tense, comparing everything that comes along in terms of something that came along before.

It takes a lot to maintain these routines. Every time you react to a circumstance in a typical way, you invest your energy in that direction. Let's say you dislike airplanes, and someone offers you a ride on an airplane. In considering the offer, you reinvest energy in your opinion about airplanes. You assure yourself that you still dislike airplanes, and politely refuse the offer.

However, going around and trying to do all of the things that you normally don't do won't help either, because in your current state that would only do harm. You would invest even more energy in trying to overcome your routine reactions and end up worse off than you began. This is the reason for secluding yourself—so that you do not have to invest energy in these routines. By ceasing to react to the world in a routine way, your overall energy levels increase to the point where even things you never believed were possible can occur.

The problem is that these routines are so insidious that you will probably find it hard to recognize them. True, cigarettes, alcohol, and drugs can all be habits or routines, but they are really just the tip of the iceberg. The time you like breakfast, your favorite socks, your thoughts on international politics, how much you love the sunset—these are all merely routines. You may think those are the endearing parts of your personality, but you probably picked them up from other people. You imitate your parents, your friends, your enemies, and your lovers. Have you ever noticed yourself saying some phrase or using some gesture that your current sexual partner always uses? You're probably not even conscious of when you began to do it.

For the period of the Abramelin operation, keep everything as fresh as possible. It will do no good to battle with these habits. Instead, recognize that you are adhering to a routine, and you will diffuse its power by being aware of it.

When you get seriously involved in your practices, you will discover that it becomes easier for you to do your work at the appointed times everyday. This is a real danger period, because your work will have become a routine. You discover that whatever your method of prayer is, it has become something that you do almost automatically.

Your work must not become a habit, a dull repetition; it must continue to be a spontaneous quest for universal awareness. You need to remain within the present every time you are practicing, focusing all of your energy in the moment. Thinking about yesterday, tomorrow, or what you are going to eat when you're done will consume all of your energy, and your efforts will be fruitless.

The Dark Night of the Soul

You must realize a fearful fact right from the beginning of the Abramelin operation. Sooner or later, you will have to face "the dark night of the soul." This phrase, first used by St. John of the Cross, refers to a condition that occurs in the mystic process in which you feel totally devoid of spiritual ability or any sense of inner light. It usually refers to an experience that you have after an extended period of doing your practice, once you have started to feel some kind of positive result. Suddenly, the positive results disappear, and you begin to feel lost in darkness and spiritual dryness.

Miguel de Molinos states that this darkness is actually God's way of drawing you in. He believes that it is necessary for the ideas and personality of the aspirant to withdraw so that God may do the instructing. "So in the beginning, when God intends to guide the Soul by an extraordinary manner into the school of the divine and loving notices of the internal law, he makes it go with darkness, and dryness, so that he may bring it near to himself."[4]

There is an old saying that the first step on the spiritual path is one into pure darkness. That is because the spiritual path leads you into your internal world and the darkness that you find there is the chaos of your own mind. At first, you may be so enthusiastic about your practices that you will not notice any darkness. It may seem as if your Angel is only inches away, as if you are almost done before you have really begun. Very quickly, this enthusiasm will falter, and you will doubt everything. It will feel as if you have lost not only that spiritual light you thought you were getting so close to, but all of the light in your life. All of this is the dark night of the soul.

This is a totally natural process. Any activity that you undertake will have this dark phase. Whether you are invoking your Holy Guardian Angel, starting to exercise, or writing a play, after a short while you will find it acutely painful to continue. Only by suffering through this darkness and letting the things that are holding you back drop away can you succeed in completing your project.

The darkness will usually manifest as a loathing for the project, a feeling that you are getting nowhere, and doubt that there is really anywhere to go. You may feel as if you are losing your mind. You may feel like you are actually becoming a much worse person than you were when you started off.

What this darkness truly consists of is all of your internal conflicts and fears that you have kept quietly at bay by building a wall between yourself and the universe. By looking within yourself, you are forced to confront these fears, and if you do not approach this operation with all of your will, you will be consumed by these fears. Only by quietly facing each of your fears, doubts, and delusions with intelligence, perseverance, courage, and silence can you succeed through this critical stage.

You may not recognize that you have entered the dark night of the soul until it completely surrounds you. It may begin as a mild boredom, or a creeping doubt, but quickly it will turn into panic and perhaps even a feeling of madness.

This is just part of the spiritual growing process. At some point, we each have to go through a period of tribulation. It happens in mundane situations too. Any learning process involves this period of dryness and anguish. Think back to when you learned the multiplication tables. At first, maybe it seemed fun, then horrible, like a looming beast, and then you were its master.

This is when the oath that you took at the beginning becomes important. You must look at that oath, and recognize that you are going through darkness, but only by adhering to the oath can you hope to reach the light.

There is another old saying that once you take a single step onto the spiritual path you are compelled to walk its entire length. This is also very true. If you abandon your practices in the middle, before you complete the operation, you will remain subject to all of the mental chaos that you've unearthed. Eventually, you will most likely manage to force it all back down into the shadows, but you may never take another step on that path. Once you begin this operation, you must succeed, or you may never succeed.

Just remember that you are seeking your Holy Guardian Angel. You cannot force this Angel to come to you; you must just be patient. Allow your fears and doubts to enter your consciousness, because you will face every one of them in one way or another before your Holy Guardian Angel will appear. Forgive yourself for having these fears, and let them quietly slink away. Eventually, they will not trouble you any longer, and you can be assured that your Angel is only moments away.

PART II

Calling Down the Divine

Methods for the Attainment 6

In essence, any method can produce the Knowledge and Conversation of your Holy Guardian Angel if you follow it with intention and perseverance. Any method intended to send you down the spiritual path will eventually lead to the goal. Some teachers will tell you to do a certain breathing technique, or a certain mantra. Others will tell you to say a certain prayer. Still others will teach you visualization techniques or some combination of all of the above. These seemingly different paths will lead to the same source, just as all rivers eventually flow to the sea. The specific technique that you use is immaterial. Most methods will require equal amounts of work in the end, even if one seems easier or harder in the beginning.

At first glance, the Abramelin method seems so simple that it almost defies belief. A person merely has to pray a couple of times daily for a few months, and at the end of that time they will walk away with the Knowledge and Conversation of their Holy Guardian Angel and a host of magical powers. On the other hand, praying and retirement can be difficult in and of themselves, and truly should not be dismissed as "simple." Not all of us have a nature that is devotional enough to engage fully in praying to a deity for six months with the hope of achieving anything. Many modern magicians don't believe in God in any conventional sense of the term. For most, simple prayer would just be empty words, even if they were trying to use the axiom, "belief is a tool." Luckily, you don't have to approach prayer in any conventional sense in order to achieve the desired results. As J. F. C. Fuller put it, "In some cases hostility to prayer would prove more fruitful than devotion to it. He who believes in denying and blaspheming God will attain to the Divine Vision of Adonai as speedily as he who believes in praying to Him and worshipping His Holy Name; so long as he 'enflame' himself with blasphemy and denial. It is the 'will' to accomplish, to conquer and overcome, which in both cases carries with it the supreme reward, and not the mere fact of denying or believing, which are but instruments towards this end."[1] In other words, the way to attain this Knowledge and Conversation with your Angel is to will it to be so and to carry that will through to the very end, no matter what may stand in your way on the path.

In chapters 7 through 14, we will discuss various methods of attainment that many people have used over the years with the greatest results. I humbly yet frankly suggest that you choose one as your primary method, but feel free to change it to suit you. In fact, you may find that a combination of the methods is the best way for you to proceed. When you first begin your practice, you may want to experiment with as many different techniques as interest you. In time, the "right" one will simply come to you. I asked my Angel if he could somehow teach me the best way to communicate with him, and I eventually received a very simple and practical method—it just sort of came to me. I'm sure you can succeed in the same way. Once you establish your methods, stick with them, and be consistent on how you combine them. Feel free to add improvements as you go along, but if you switch from ecstatic dancing to seated mantra chanting after you've established the former as your invocation method, you are likely to lose a lot of ground. Switching methods like this becomes a real danger during the dark night of the soul. Once you have gotten that far, changing what you are doing might negate all of the work that you have already done.

In terms of the exact practices you adopt, be creative, and do not restrict yourself to the letter of anything in this or any other book. You will naturally find ways of improving these practices for yourself, and you should make those changes as you like.

These practices are means to an end. Do not become lost in endless details, or you will lose any chance of achieving your goal. Some people get so involved in these practices that they forget what the goal is, thinking that the steps in the practices themselves are the important thing. They become lost in endless detail and get nothing at all done in the end. A lot of people also seem to think that there is one "right" method of attaining any magical or mystical experience, and I assure you that this is total nonsense. By showing you a wide selection of perfectly valid methods to examine and choose from, I hope you will be able to see the bigger picture. There are an infinite number of ways of gaining the Knowledge and Conversation of your Holy Guardian Angel, but we can adequately describe only a few within the confines of a single book.

The methods that I will discuss in the following chapters are:

Yoga techniques; ceremonial magick rituals; The ש of ש Operation; astral travel, or "rising on the planes;" devotion and prayer; awareness and Zen; and sexual techniques.

Remember that each of these methods will lead to the highest results if you use them correctly. They all have the potential to lead to that heavenly vision of your Holy Guardian Angel. If you abuse any of these techniques, or mistake them for the end, they will only lead you into delusion. You should also remember that there are many other methods you can use, and you should not feel restricted in any way.

However, in terms of approaching your practice—no matter what your path—you should adhere to the basic rules I detailed previously and summarize here:

❋ Commit to performing your practice every single day, no matter what it is. This may make one or another technique more appropriate to your lifestyle.

❋ You must have a dedicated space, a temple that has an altar on which to burn incense. Each time you perform your practice, you should burn the special Abramelin incense described on page 27. The incense will have a cumulative effect on your consciousness, and you should not omit it. Your sense of smell automatically triggers your brain to enter the states to which the scent is associated.

❋ You should incorporate into your life the purifications, consecrations, and Eucharist described in chapter 4 as much as possible.

If you sincerely adopt these few, simple things, being sure to perform a practice session daily, you will achieve the highest result.

Yoga Techniques 7

The word *yoga* means "union." It is derived from the same root as our English word *yoke*. In other words, the science of yoga involves joining things together. At its core, yoga is a very precise system for controlling the mind in order to facilitate unity consciousness. This unity consciousness is called *samadhi*.

According to Aleister Crowley, etymologically, the word *samadhi* is composed of the roots *sam* (Greek: ΣΥΜ), which means "together with," and *adhi* (Hebrew: א [Adonai]), which means "the Lord," the Personal Lord, or Holy Guardian Angel. In other words, samadhi is the Knowledge and Conversation of the Holy Guardian Angel.[1] An Indian yogi might not entirely agree, but in our Western, syncretic culture, I assure you that this is true. The goal of yoga is the same as any form of Western mysticism: to become one with God. There are many different kinds of yoga, but the one that concerns us at present, the one that will lead to our goal, is Raja Yoga, the yoga of will.

There are several pieces that fit together to form this practice, so this book can only give an outline. However, you will certainly be able to get started, and will know everything that you need to know to accomplish the end. If you wish to gain a more comprehensive knowledge of yoga, the works of Swami Vivakananda[2] or Aleister Crowley's writings on yoga[3] would form an excellent place to start.

While the methods I teach in this chapter are by no means the traditional teachings of the East, they are a distillation of the practical fruits of the philosophy. These practices are based primarily on the writings of Aleister Crowley, who synthesized many yoga practices into his system of attainment.

The purpose of the yoga practices in this chapter is to assist you in the process of meditating. When you first try to meditate, it almost seems like a hopeless cause. You cannot relax, focus, or do anything but fret. In order to attain samadhi—unity consciousness—you must struggle past a lot of resistance from every part of your being.

First, there is the matter of your body. As you try to contemplate your Angel, you itch, your back aches, the messages from your body constantly disrupt your concentration. To fight this, you, as the would-be yogi must sit still in an *asana*. This is a special position that you sit in until you no longer find it uncomfortable to do so. Once you have mastered your asana, your body will no longer disturb your meditation.

Second, there is the matter of your emotions. As you try to contemplate your Angel, you are distracted by doubts, fears that people will think you are crazy for wasting your time like this, or thoughts about the beautiful person you saw at the grocery store. Psychologists and doctors have known for a long time that deep, regulated breathing calms your emotions. In fact, taking a deep breath can often shift you away from a challenging emotion entirely. This is why it is so often suggested that you "take a deep breath" when you are feeling upset. Indian yogis have been aware of this for thousands of years, and the technique they developed for this purpose is *pranayama*, which literally means "control of the breath."[4] When you have mastered pranayama, your emotions will remain calm and peaceful.

Third, there is the matter of the thinking mind. As you try to contemplate your Angel, even after you have conquered your body and your emotions, you are still distracted by a thousand thoughts running through your mind. You forget what your intentions were, and you slip off into reveries and daydreams. This problem is difficult to conquer, so the yogis developed three practices that focus on calming the mind. The first is *pratyahara*, in which you turn your mind inward, inspecting the core of your thoughts, until you can kill any thought before it even forms. The second is the *mantra*, which is a phrase that you repeat in a rhythmic fashion. This serves to slow down the mind and to focus it on the flow of the mantra. The third is *dharana*, in which you concentrate your mind on a single thought, image, or point. This is usually done either by concentrating on a holy image, or on some internal energy center in your body. The three techniques work together, or you can use them individually. However, pratyahara is a prerequisite to being able to master either of the other practices.

Once you have mastered dharana and you are able to think single-mindedly, you will experience *dhyana*. You can consider dhyana to be the single-pointed relationship between you and the object of concentration. It is the outpouring of yourself solely upon the object of concentration. When you prolong this single-pointedness until there ceases to be any difference between you and that object, you experience samadhi.

This may sound difficult, and perhaps not even that enjoyable, but success is ecstasy. It is much more powerful and beautiful than the most exhilarating sex. There is no other pleasure in this world that can compare with the union between you and your Angel. Samadhi is that union. With that brief overview, let us begin our practical approach to each subject.

Asana

The first step in this process is to sit in a position that you can maintain for an extended period without problems. There are hundreds of different asanas in the yoga philosophies, and each one is reputed to have some benefit that is either physiological or magical. In truth, any position is really okay for your goal, as long as your spine is straight and you are comfortable. You can even sit in a chair or lie on the floor.

There are two schools of thought on this subject. One says that you should assume a comfortable position so that you don't have to struggle from the very beginning to maintain it. The other says that you should assume a thoroughly uncomfortable position so that you have to concentrate in order to maintain it, and do not shift or change positions unconsciously. Both sides have a point, but the approach you want to take is really up to you.

The easiest position is to simply sit "Indian-style," or cross-legged. It is important to put enough pillows under your bottom so that you properly support your back. If you do not do this, your back will start to hurt after a very short time. Your shoulders should be slightly rolled back so that your chest is open, and your lower back should be gently pressed backward to straighten out your spine's curvature.

If you are interested in positions that are more cumbersome, consult one of the many good books that describe them. Whatever position you choose, within fifteen minutes or less of remaining still in it, the position will become incredibly uncomfortable. This is to be expected, but you should under no circumstances start shifting around. You must remain absolutely stationary, staying at ease as much as possible. Regardless of how itchy or unpleasant you feel, you should not move.

Before you sit down to practice, you should decide how long you are going to remain still, and then be sure to stay still for that period of time. Ten to fifteen minutes is probably a good start for the beginner.

As you endeavor to do this daily, it will most likely become more painful at first rather than less painful. You will begin to dread doing it. However, if you are faithful to it, there will come a day when you find that it is no longer at all uncomfortable. This will mean that you have conquered your body, and will be ready to move on to other things.[5]

Pranayama

As with asanas, there are many different kinds of pranayama, each intended to give the practitioner different magical abilities. We will concern ourselves only with the basics here. Even the simplest pranayamas have two effects. The first is the quieting of emotions; the second is of establishing a slow and easy rhythm of the bodily functions, which can allow the

mind to forget itself and achieve samadhi. In fact, quietly count-
ing the seconds as you inhale and exhale can in itself result in
samadhi. This is essentially the same as chanting any mantra.

Pranayama is extremely easy to understand. There are
three parts of pranayama practice:

Rechaka pranayama—exhaling the breath;

Puraka pranayama—inhaling the breath;

Kumbhaka pranayama—restraining the breath.

These are sometimes called the "three kings" of pranayama.
The third part, kumbakha, is credited with magical power. The
idea is that by restraining the breath, you restrain the mind, by
controlling the breath, you control the mind. By controlling the
mind, the universe disappears and anything is possible.

Pranayama Exercises

1. For the purpose of attaining the Knowledge and
    Conversation of your Angel, you need only a very
    basic technique. Simply start filling your lungs from
    the bottom, slowly expanding your diaphragm, then
    fill the middle of your lungs, and then fill your lungs
    all the way up until the air reaches your shoulders.
    Then slowly release it, until your lungs are entirely
    empty. Try to time this so that you are breathing in
    and out for the same amount of time. In other
    words, if you inhale for 10 seconds, then you should
    exhale for 10 seconds. This is one pranayama.

    If you choose to add khumbaka, retaining the
    breath, to this practice, you should start out with an

even sequence. For example, inhale for 10 seconds, retain the breath for 10 seconds, then exhale for 10 seconds. When this has become easy and pleasurable, then you can try the next two exercises.

2. Draw in your breath for 4 seconds, hold it for 16, and then exhale it for 8. This makes one pranayama. You can extend this indefinitely by adjusting the length of each breath but retaining the ratio (for instance, 8, 32, and 16 or 10, 40, and 20). At the same time, you concentrate on the muladhara chakra at the base of the spine in order to arouse the coiled power of Kundalini.

3. Assume your asana; draw in prana through the ida (left nostril), retain it until your body begins to perspire and shake, and then exhale it through pingala (right nostril) very slowly.

These are just three examples of the hundreds of different pranayama practices. The benefits of these practices will be increased energy; greater calmness; feelings of centeredness, peace, and well-being; and the ability to focus. If you are interested in pranayama, you can find a lot of information about it among the documents of the A∴ A∴—which can be found in Crowley's book, *Magic: Liber ABA, Book Four*— and in yoga treatises such as the *Hatha Yoga Pradipika* or the *Shiva Samhita*.

Mantra

Once you're accustomed to pranayama, the best way to time it is by using a mantra. Some Indian sages say that certain mantras are more suited to one person or another, and some of them charge a significant amount of money to initiate a student into the mantra that they think the student should use. I seriously wonder whether their purpose is spiritual or monetary. In my experience, it does not matter what your mantra is if it pleases you and helps you get your result.

A mantra can do for your mind what pranayama does for your breathing. Everything will slow to a natural pace, and you will find yourself focused and peaceful.

Some people say their mantra aloud; others merely say it in the mind. Experiment is your best advisor.

The mantra should have a rhythmic quality, with an emphasis on one or more syllables so you will remain relaxed and concentrated on the mantra while you are repeating it. If you are able to repeat your mantra while thinking intensely about five other things at the same time, it's not serving its purpose.

Here are some examples of Hindu mantras, but you need not feel that you must use any of them:

Aum

Aum Tat Sat Aum

Aum Mani Padme Hum

Aum Shivaya Vashi

Aum Namahe Shivaya Aum

You could even use a mantra that has something specific to do with your Angel, although it might be best if it doesn't have a great deal of meaning. You don't want to be distracted by thinking about the deep significance of your mantra, for in doing so you will be engaging your intellect.

If it's some pretty piece of Elizabethan poetry, it might get distracting. A mantra is just one of many tools for stilling the mind.

Pratyahara

After you have become proficient at pranayama—with or without the use of a mantra—you can begin the next stage of practice, pratyahara, which is the process of making the mind introspective. The purpose of this introspection is to gain control over your mind so that outside and internal influences do not disturb you, and you can block out all but the one object you are concentrating on.

The first thing to do in pratyahara is to sit and let your mind run on, observing where it is going and what it is doing. Once you become involved in this, you will realize that your mind is true chaos. You can simply watch this chaos as a dispassionate observer, focusing on the way that your thoughts are proceeding. As the thoughts go through your head like clouds blowing by, you will notice that there many different kinds of thought. Some thoughts will be louder than others, and some thoughts will be like pictures. You will also notice that some of the thoughts that you hear do not seem to come from your consciousness at all, and may not have anything to do with you—these are strange, but mostly gibberish. As the loudest thoughts quiet down under your casual observation, you will start to notice deeper thoughts that were previously subconscious.

Once you begin to notice these root thoughts, you can start to check them as they begin, strangling them before they can be born. You should by no means attempt to check your thoughts until you have achieved the state of noticing these root thoughts. If you try to battle the loudest thoughts, you will only excite your mind even more. After you have become proficient at observing your thoughts, and checking them before they begin, you can move on to the next stage, dharana.

Dharana

Dharana is the practice of focusing the mind on a single object pictured in the mind. This is the practice most likely to lead to samadhi, although mantra chanting or even pranayama might yield samadhi if carried far enough. The object of your concentration can either be a symbol—religious or otherwise—or even a part of the body, but it must be singular. Since you are practicing this in order to attain your Angel, it might be appropriate to choose something that relates to that subject. For instance, you could concentrate on the crown of your head, the sahasrara chakra, which is the location of the connection between the human mind and the divine. You could focus on the third eye, or ajna chakra, where kundalini Shakti and Shiva join. You could focus on an image of a golden hexagram, which is an abstract Qabalistic symbol of your Holy Guardian Angel. You could also focus on a cross, or an eye in a triangle.

Although this exercise may seem simple, as soon as you begin, you will find that it is almost impossible to hold an image steady in your mind. The shape of the object will change. It will entirely disappear. Competing images will suddenly come in front of the object of your concentration. Frequently, you will go for long periods having forgotten your intention completely, and thinking about something else.

Each of these disturbances is called a "break." At first, you will probably have more breaks than moments of concentration. The only way to battle this is with practice. In order to discover whether you are making progress, count the number of breaks that you have in each practice period. The easiest way to do this is with a string of beads. Each time you notice a break, simply shift a bead over on the string. That way, you will be able to keep track of how many breaks you have without having to think about it, which would just cause more breaks. Eventually, you will have a very special kind of break, which will be the indication that you have achieved dhyana.

Dhyana

Different teachers use dhyana in different ways, but for our purposes, we shall consider it as the precursor to the goal of samadhi. When dhyana occurs, it is a spasm of the mind. In essence, it is the result of successful dharana, so all that exists in the mind is the object of concentration. This sounds mundane, but it is actually quite a profound experience. Everything else simply disappears, and all that remains is the connection between you and the object of concentration. The effect is so shocking that it can last for only a moment the first time you experience it. But even this moment seems eternal.

Samadhi

Finally, we come to samadhi. Samadhi is the state of unity consciousness. You have become so at one with the object of your concentration that you have both ceased to exist. It is not that you have become the Holy Guardian Angel, or that the Angel has filled you. Samadhi is the destruction of your previous experience of you. You will not experience yourself at all in samadhi. Unity is the only way to describe this experience in positive terms, but it is not accurate. "Without difference" would be a closer description, but that hardly makes sense.

The three experiences—dharana, dhyana, and samadhi—really are one process. Every one of the practices in this book will lead to these three states. Regardless of how you approach the Abramelin operation, samadhi and the Knowledge and Conversation of your Holy Guardian Angel are essentially the same. All of the practices in this book require some form of concentration (dharana) and when this concentration, is perfected, it becomes dhyana (perfect concentration), and then samadhi (the Knowledge and Conversation of your Holy Guardian Angel). Whether or not you plan to use yoga as your way to attainment, you would be wise to familiarize yourself with the basics of these exercises, because in one way or another, they will all prove invaluable to you.

Ceremonial Magick 8

Modern ceremonial magick is based on a Western spiritual tradition that is thousands of years old. Most of the symbolism and ritual comes from Egyptian, Greek, Hebrew, and Chaldean sources, and represents the somewhat fractured legacy of these initiatory traditions. Astrology, alchemy, tarot divination, and most New Age philosophies are in some way or another the children of this vast tradition. The author of *The Abramelin* has some strong opinions about certain types of magick, which seem more like personal and medieval prejudices than any kind of real advice. However, the basis of his statements is that ceremony is but a pale imitation of truth. It is possible to invoke powers ceremonially while not truly invoking them in your heart. This seems to be the core of the author's complaint, and I wholeheartedly agree with his sentiment. However, just because it is possible to perform ceremonies emptily does not mean that we should dismiss them.

There are many varieties of modern ceremonial magick. There is Hebrew Qabalistic magick, hermetic magick, planetary magick, elemental magick, and witchcraft. Even these rather broad categories have many subcategories, and all tend to blend one into another. The subject is far too wide for the limits of this book. The basic structure of magical ritual and how it might relate to your quest for the Holy Guardian Angel is what really interests us here. A magical ritual is a series of actions intended to bring about a specific change in one's current conditional reality. For instance, someone might perform a ritual to bring rain, or wealth, or a love affair.

Since we humans are tiny and insignificant creatures, we cannot do many things without the assistance of "invisible forces," which we can invoke to bring about changes that are beyond our conscious control. However, we need to find a way to tell these invisible forces what we want them to do. The manner that the ancients adopted was to suppose that visible things that were similar in nature to the invisible forces (which they personified as gods, angels, and demons) would attract them. For instance, they decided that gold was of the same character as the Sun. So, when they wanted to attract a solar invisible force, they involved gold in some way in the process.

Eventually, a complex series of correspondences[1] developed, in which the letters of the alphabet, colors, numbers, names, abstract symbols, and different movements of the body could be used to attract and control different invisible forces. This is the basis of all magical ritual. The people who developed this process were, for the most part, not using anything like modern scientific methods. What they were doing was going inside their minds, and developing these techniques from the archetypes of the unconscious. They were developing a relationship with the universe based on the human mind. They dealt with these forces on an extremely personal level, naming them and describing their appearance when they manifested a personified form.

You could say that the process of contacting spirits in the mind is merely imaginary, and that would be true in one sense, but the process involved is valid in terms of the human mind. Whether results can be achieved on the physical plane is based on how well you are actually able to connect to these universal invisible forces and make them work on whatever your target is.

Traditionally, there are two ways of getting the invisible forces to do what you want once you have contacted them. The first is to make a deal with them. This is what sacrificial types of magick are about. You offer the spirits what they want—some blood or your soul—and they give you what you want. This is really the lowest kind of magick and is usually attempted with so-called "evil" spirits, the devils, demons, and elemental creatures of the world. This is because for the most part the "good" spirits don't have an interest in blood or souls. The theory is that evil spirits are low and good spirits high on the ladder of consciousness, with humans right in the middle. So, by making deals with these lower spirits, we are letting them enjoy things that are higher than they are.

The second way of getting the spirits to work for us is to get in touch with their superiors. These are the spirits that are higher up on the spiritual scale, the gods and angels. The way that we do this is by invoking them, filling our hearts and minds with the qualities of these higher beings until we obtain their identities. Instead of offering something that we may or may not need in the future—an animal or our soul—we actually offer ourselves up into the ecstasy of union with this celestial being, that it might deign to become one with us. The idea is that by obtaining identity with a spirit that rules over a lot of other spirits, we then get rule of an entire army of spirits. This process requires much more work than the first, but it is the most valuable in terms of the Knowledge and Conversation of the Holy Guardian Angel. In fact, the Holy Guardian Angel is our connection to the highest universal power, so by attaining identity with our Angel, we actually gain dominion over all of creation.

Now, the question is: How do we create a ritual that will have this effect? The way that the ancients conceived the matter was very similar to the principles that I discuss throughout this book.

In order to get in contact with any force, it is first necessary to purify the working area of anything unrelated to that force. Very often, magicians work in small circles, because this is a very easy way to delineate the working area from the non-working area. The circle is also a symbol that represents the universe, because it is unbroken and has no edges, beginning, or end. The magical circle is like a private universe, or microcosm, for you to work in. Around the edges of the circle, you write the most powerful names of God, ones that will keep all evil spirits from daring to enter the circle without permission. These names of God are entirely personal, depending on your philosophy and belief system. Examples can be found in most ancient magick books such as *The Lesser Key of Solomon*.

Now, even though the circle has been emptied of all but the essentials, and the names of God have been written around it, there may be some spirits (those who can't read, for instance) still floating around in the circle. In order to get rid of these spirits, you need to perform a short banishing ritual in order to let the spirits know that you are serious. This sort of ritual usually involves calling down the power of the highest, and then shouting powerful names of God at the four quarters of the universe. One of the most commonly used rituals is "The Lesser Banishing Ritual of the Pentagram."[2] It is a ritual from the Hermetic Order of the Golden Dawn, and can be found in most books that teach the basics of ceremonial magick. I have also included a version of it below.

The Lesser Banishing Ritual of the Pentagram

1. Touching your forehead, say *Ateh* (Unto Thee).

2. Touching your chest, say *Malkuth* (The Kingdom).

3. Touching your right shoulder, say *ve-Geburah* (and the Power).

4. Touching your left shoulder, say *ve-Gedulah* (and the Glory).

5. Clasping your hands upon your chest, say *le-Olahm, Amen* (To the Ages, Amen).

6. Turning to the East, trace the Earth pentagram with your finger or your weapon (usually the wand). Say sonorously (i.e., vibrate) *I H V H*. (Pronounced as "Ye-ho-wau.")

7. Turning to the South, trace the pentagram, and vibrate *A D N I*. (Pronounced as "Adonai.")

8. Turning to the West, trace the pentagram and vibrate *A H I H*. (Pronounced as "Eheieh.")

9. Turning to the North, trace the pentagram and vibrate *A G L A.* (Pronounced as "Agla.") Pronounce: Ye-ho-wau, Adonai, Eheieh, Agla.

10. Extending your arms to form a Cross, say:

11. Before me Raphael;

12. Behind me Gabriel;

13. On my right hand Michael.

14. On my left hand Auriel;

15. For about me flames the Pentagram,

16. And in the Column stands the six-rayed Star.

17. Repeat steps 1 to 5, the Qabalistic Cross.[3]

After you are sure that all the stray spirits are outside the circle, you must formally purify and consecrate your working temple. You do this by sprinkling water and censing the borders of your magical circle or area. You perform this with the appropriate words.

Then you swear an oath that you will complete the operation and that you will not stop until you have completed it. (See p. 39 for the specifics on oaths.)

After your oath-taking, you may commence your invocations. You can perform the invocation with words, dance, symbols, or some combination thereof or any other means that you think will help you achieve your goal. The point is to attain a union with whatever it is that you are invoking, so whatever means you use should be in harmony with whatever you are invoking. Since your invocation will be of your Holy Guardian Angel, your invocation should be related in some way to the highest principles you can conceive of and beyond.

The Lesser Banishing Ritual of the Pentagram above could actually serve as your entire ceremony in this case, since it contains within itself an oath, an invocation of the highest, and a balancing of the elements. Of this ritual's real significance, Aleister Crowley once said, "Those who regard this ceremony as a mere device to invoke or banish spirits, are unworthy to possess it. Properly understood, it is the Medicine of the Metals and the Stone of the Wise."[4] This high praise is, indeed, appropriate from Crowley, but the ritual that he used to invoke his Angel is really just an extended variation along the same theme. Crowley's ritual was actually built upon the Bornless Ritual, into which he combined elements of the pentagram ritual. The Bornless Ritual contains long strings of barbarous syllables that he recited as he imagined his consciousness expanding. He performed the whole ritual astrally, imagining himself expanding into the four directions of the elements, and then upward toward the element of spirit.[5] If you were going to use the Lesser Banishing Ritual of the Pentagram as your whole invocation, you would need to work very slowly, visualizing the appropriate images vividly, particularly at the beginning and the end.

You are probably better off making up your own ritual than trying to imitate ones such as Aleister Crowley's Bornless Ritual. Your magical rituals must make sense to you, as well as have great personal meaning for you, or they will do you no good. Using the basic tools in Crowley's "Liber O"[6] combined with your own creativity, you can design a ritual that will be appropriate for you.

The important thing to remember when performing magick is that you are not merely saying things and doing things.

You need to engage your whole being in your rituals, or they will be useless. If you are calling down universal energies, you must really call them down. This is an act of imagination, but it is also more than that. It is magick. You are not really getting it right until the energy seems to flow on its own, with you acting as a conductor. It may take a number of experiments to discover this energy, and it will take a significant amount of time to be its master.

Ceremonial magick is tremendously potent for some people, but it is not for everyone. It requires a very active imagination, and the ability to lose yourself to forces that are not directly related to your consciousness while you are moving around and speaking. If you are unable to lose yourself in action in this way, there are many other ways that you can approach the Knowledge and Conversation of your Holy Guardian Angel. Magick has many faces and many forms. You will find your perfect expression only through experiment and exploration.

Astral Travel 9

The astral plane is the realm from which the "spirits" of magick come. You could say that it is an imaginary place, but that would be stripping it of its true importance. It is the place where the human mind comprehends the world without the interference of the intellect. It is the home of the "collective unconscious," where angels, devils, and gods are perfectly real. Dismissing such a place as simply "imaginary" is misunderstanding its power. The forces of the astral plane move the world both socially and spiritually. Poets, religious leaders, musicians, artists, and even many politicians draw their power from this realm of dreams and inspiration.

Astral travel is the art of traveling to this ephemeral world. It involves creating an imaginary body and transferring your consciousness to that body which you then use to travel to various locations. Now, you could argue that anything that you meet that way is going to be only in your mind, but you would also have to admit that mathematics exists "only in your mind." You most likely wouldn't argue that mathematics is useless, and it would be silly to argue that astral traveling is useless until you have experimented with it. The fact that something exists "in your mind" does not negate its validity. You will eventually discover that this astral world is just as real a place as the physical world. It is just the conditions of its reality that are different.

You would be best off experimenting with this technique only after you have become familiar with both some yoga and some magical ritual. Perform a banishing ritual before the experiment, or do something of the nature of banishing in order to concentrate your mind and free the working area of "wandering spirits." You should do this experiment in a darkened room. Of course, your temple would be the best place.

The Basic Technique

Sit in a position in which you can remain comfortably still. In order to begin your astral travel, you need to separate your astral body from your physical one. One of the easiest ways to do this is to close your eyes and imagine a form in front of you that resembles yourself. Try to get as clear an image as you can, but don't worry about it too much. Now shift your perspective around and imagine how your physical body looks from the perspective of this imaginary body. Attempt to transfer as much of your consciousness as possible to this imaginary body, and then look around at the rest of your environment from this new perspective. When you feel fairly comfortable doing this, rise up into the air, and continue to rise until you begin to see things. You will be on the hinterlands of the astral plane.

Experiment with this practice several times, until it becomes quite easy and natural for you separate your consciousness from your body and travel into this new realm. It shouldn't take long before you realize that you have actually shifted all of your consciousness into this other body and have had many interesting experiences.

At this point, you can begin to experiment with combining magical ritual with this practice and observe the results. Try invoking some force using the techniques in Crowley's "Liber O" and chapter 8. Then travel upward in your astral body until you discover a vision. Compare your vision with the forces you have invoked. If you have been working properly, there should be a noticeable correspondence.

Rising on the Planes

Once you are familiar with the astral plane, you can begin actually using your new skill to gain the Knowledge and Conversation of your Holy Guardian Angel. Astral travel by itself will most likely not lead to any really important experiences, but by using the basic technique in a slightly different way, you can turn it into a simple and powerful invocation of your Holy Guardian Angel. This corollary technique to astral travel is called "rising on the planes." Rising on the planes starts out in exactly the same way as astral travel; you separate from your physical body and rise in the air, but this time you continue to rise and don't stop for any reason. Make sure that you continue to travel straight upward. If you begin to see images, beings, or landscapes, simply ignore them and continue to rise. You will most likely become confused or fatigued or distracted, but through it all, just continue to rise. If you continue at this without stopping for any reason, you can reach samadhi, the Knowledge and Conversation of your Holy Guardian Angel.

Rising on the planes is probably the most straightforward way to achieve success, but it can also lead you astray, because once you begin working at this practice, you will see myriad angels, devils, and buddhas, all of which will be vying for your belief that they are your Angel. Believing any of these to be your Angel would be just about the worst mistake you could make. These astral phantoms would be more than happy to pretend at being your Angel for quite some time, and would gleefully lead you off into a world of bigotry, delusion, and madness. This often happens to the "rabid evangelical"[1] type of personality. Some demon masquerades as their God and fills their head with every kind of abomination imaginable. I have met many magicians whose "angels" help them to excuse neglecting their relationships and children, serious drug abuse, and general mental disease. Please steer clear of this type of "angel." Do not confuse your neuroses with your Holy Guardian Angel.

The way to avoid this is quite simple—by discerning the nature of your contact with the being. The confrontation with your Angel will be a Transformation. It will be as if an electric shock blasted through your spine, disintegrating you into a hundred billion pieces and spreading them across the whole universe and at the same time feel like the warmest, coziest snuggle in the fluffiest downy bed you could imagine. You will not be the same after the experience. While you are enjoying the Conversation of your Angel, you will no longer exist as you currently conceive of yourself. You will then feel like you know a secret that everybody knows if only they could realize it. The specifics of your experience may vary to some degree, but I think you can see what I'm getting at. Any relationship you form with a spirit that does not possess this quality of transformation and power is not the Knowledge and Conversation of your Angel. With this small warning, you can safely proceed into the fantastic realm of the astral plane.[2]

The שׁ of שׁ Operation 10

The letter שׁ, pronounced "shin," is the Hebrew letter for the sound "sh." In Qabalistic symbolism, this letter signifies the spirit element. The Shin of Shin Operation is a ritual formula based on the Hermetic Order of the Golden Dawn's Neophyte ritual. The purpose of the Shin of Shin ritual is to obtain the Knowledge and Conversation of the Holy Guardian Angel.

For simplicity, the Shin of Shin Operation can be reduced to a series of mental operations that result in the same effect. Magick need not be complicated in order to work.

Performing the שׁ of שׁ Operation

I highly recommend that you begin this practice by performing a banishing ritual and then a self-purification and consecration.

Sit in a position in which you can remain comfortably still.

Close your eyes and imagine that your body is a black egg.[1] It should be a deep, flat black, like absolute emptiness.

Imagine that you are floating above a black sea. On your left is a giant pillar made of cloud. On your right, a giant pillar of fire. The two pillars descend deep into the darkness below you, and rise up into the heavens infinitely far above you. The left pillar represents the mercy and love of the universe, and the right pillar represents the severity and cruelty of the universe.

To equilibrate these two opposites, imagine a point of divine white brilliance above you, shining down on your egg. This is the descent of unity and holiness, the descent of your Angel. Pause and feel the two pillars and the light above.

Between you and this holiness, imagine a flashing sword that is like lightning. Aspire toward the light with all your power, push all of your personal energy up through your spine (you are still a black egg, however), toward the point of light, keeping your attention on the flashing sword. The more you push toward the light, the closer the flashing sword comes to you. As you push with all of your might toward the light, imagine the flashing sword descending upon you and striking you on the back of your neck, the shock and pain of which destroys your conscious personality. Pause and feel your emptiness. The two pillars and the white light are still there.

The holy light then sends a ray of light down upon you, spiraling around your egg three times, and your egg turns gray from this influx of light. Pause and feel the small amount of light within you.

The holy light descends upon you again, spiraling around your egg three times, until your egg is nearly white.

Aspire again toward the light with all your power, push all of your personal energy up through your spine toward this light, keeping your attention on the flashing sword that is still before you. The more you push toward the light, the closer the flashing sword comes to you. As you push with all of your might toward the light, imagine the flashing sword descending upon you, and striking you on the back of your neck, destroying you again.

This time, a giant pyramid of flame appears in the midst of the divine light above you. You feel the light filling you, and the fire growing brighter.

Withdraw for a moment, and assure yourself that the two pillars still remain at your sides, then with all of your might aspire to and invoke the light and fire that is above you, and allow all to disintegrate into this infinite, boundless light.

It will probably take a bit of time for this operation to have an impact on you. The advantage of this technique is that it operates in pure symbols and has no dogmatic implications. It is a very beautiful and powerful meditation.

If this formula appeals to you, but you would like to do it as a ritual, simply act out the components within a magical circle. This exercise in any form would also be a perfect supplement to a magical or a yoga practice. It could be the whole of your practice if you wish.

Devotion 11

D evotion is probably the best method for obtaining a vision of divine grace and presence. I doubt that any of the other methods could work without a kernel of devotion inside of you. If you are a devout believer in a religion, or if you happen to feel that devotion and prayer could be useful for you, then you have a perfect means for concentrating toward the end of attaining to your Angel. It really doesn't matter what god you pray to, as long as it is one about which you feel strongly. The god that you pray to should, in some way, represent your highest concepts of the universe. You should invoke a holy presence that is complete. For example, Aphrodite, although a wonderful goddess, represents only one aspect of godhead. Pray directly to your Holy Guardian Angel if you want to make things simple.

This method is so uncomplicated that it hardly needs elaboration, and if you carry it through with sincerity and dedication, it will certainly lead to success. The secret is, of course, to "enflame yourself with praying." As long as you pray with your heart, from the center of your being, the gateway will eventually burst open, and you will have the Knowledge and Conversation of your Angel.

If there is an image appropriate to your deity, you should hang it prominently in your temple so it can inspire you. It should be as beautiful an image of your deity as you are capable of obtaining. Also, you must be sure that while you are conducting the operation your way of life is such that it will please your particular deity. In other words, you must be sinless in the eyes of your god, and the requirements for that state vary depending on what god you are serving.

In essence, all you then need to do is to go into your temple once or twice a day, and pray with all your heart to your deity or your Angel. If you passionately follow this through for a period of time, you will eventually receive a divine visitation. It may come as illumination, a vision, or instruction on what you should do next in order to obtain your Holy Guardian Angel. This could be a precarious experience, as it is possible for a fantasy or delusion to take the place of your god and give you horrible advice, which could be dangerous if you are a reactionary or easily influenced person. If you use common sense, you'll save yourself a lot of trouble. If gentle Jesus tells you to go out and kill homeless people or doctors at abortion clinics, you're probably not talking to Jesus.

Aleister Crowley outlines a complete system of devotion in his *Liber Astarte*. The basics are pretty much the same as what I've outlined above. However, in the instructions he gives a full formula for a prayer that you may find useful. It is by no means necessary, but you can use it if you like. This prayer has seven parts, because seven is the Qabalistic number of love. Its structure is as follows:

First, a confession and supplication, as a slave unto his Lord.

Second, an Oath, as a vassal to his Liege.

Third, a Memorial, as of a child to his Parent.

Fourth, an Orison, as of a Priest unto his God.

Fifth, a Colloquy, as of a Brother with his Brother.

Sixth, a Conjuration, as to a Friend with his Friend.

Seventh, a Madrigal, as of a Lover to his Mistress.

The first should be of awe, the second of fealty, the third of dependence, the fourth of adoration, the fifth of confidence, the sixth of comradeship, the seventh of passion.[1]

If a formal and prewritten prayer seems overcomplicated or unnatural, you could simply pray extemporaneously, something new and unique each time. Just remember to fill your prayer with passion. Your passion must build up until it is finally capable of carrying you beyond yourself; this is essential in any method.

Sexual Techniques 12

S ex and religion have always had a strong relationship, but this has often been swept under the rug of conservative morals, or kept behind the closed doors of the inner sanctuaries of secret initiatory societies.

Tantric Yoga, Gnostic Christianity, the Cult of Priapus, Voodoo, Sufism—these all possess sexual methods for attaining union with the divine. In many ways, sex is probably the easiest way of achieving results, because it is naturally ecstatic, and its effect upon consciousness is so instantaneous and profound. In his small but fascinating book, *A Manual of Sex Magick*, Louis Culling describes a very interesting way of contacting your Holy Guardian Angel. He outlines three separate degrees of sex magick. The first is called Alphaism. In this stage, you practice "magical chastity." This is not traditional chastity. There is no prohibition of sex at all, except that all sexual intercourse must be within the

context of a sex magical rite. Once you have begun magical
chastity, all of your sex life is devoted to magick. What's
more, you have "no emotions about sex between the occasions of sexual congrex."[1] The only time that your mind is
allowed to indulge in sexual thoughts at all is when you are
conducting a sex magick rite. You could perform sex magick
every day, but between sex acts, you have to keep it out of
your mind. This seems very hard, but you could try!

This "magical chastity" continues into the practices of the
second and third degree. The second degree is called
"Dianism." In this degree, you enjoy sexual intercourse without climaxing. This degree holds the most interest in terms of
the Angel. The basic way to conduct a second degree sex magick ritual is to approach your lover as if he or she is the physical embodiment or avatar of your Angel. To effectively achieve
this feeling, you remove the "lower personality" of your lover
from your mind. Your lover must become to you that divine
lover, your Holy Guardian Angel. Because of this, Dianic sex
magick rites should be performed in darkness and there should
be no verbal communication between the participants, unless
it is to recite an invocation or the rubric of a ritual. Once you
begin the sexual act, delight in the feeling of ecstasy, don't
avoid it. However, rather than losing yourself to the ecstasy of
sex, use it to fire an energized enthusiasm toward achieving the
Knowledge and Conversation of your Angel. The more you
invest this sexual energy into your Angel, the more powerful
the impact of the act will be. The whole thing should be done
slowly and with ease, there should be no rushing for either
partner, since no climax is intended. The result of this practice
is supposed to be astounding and cumulative.

The third degree is, in scheme, the same as the second,
except that at the end, after an extremely prolonged period of

sex (no less than an hour) orgasm is achieved, and the resulting fluid of the union is either used to consecrate a talisman or consumed as a Eucharist.

You could easily use these sexual concepts along with the ש of ש Operation, devotions, or yoga techniques to achieve an even more profound impact. Sex magick rituals can fill you with a passion to experience even more ecstasy, to make that divine union complete. Of course, it is important that you have your partner's cooperation and that s/he can keep up with you!

It is also possible to use autoeroticism, or masturbation, in a similar way to fan the flames of your angelic passion. To do this you would extend your stimulation over a long period, attempting to draw yourself closer and closer to your Angel as you bring yourself closer and closer to orgasm. The key to using sexuality as a gateway to the divine is the use of attention. In the beginning, you need to give your attention to something arousing. If you are aroused by your Angel, then focusing your attention will be easy, but chances are this abstract concept will not turn you on sexually. Because of this, it is permissible to focus on your partner or fantasize a sexually tantalizing image until you begin to feel orgasm is imminent. At that point, refocus your attention on union with your Angel. Extend and expand this near-orgasmic period of focusing on your angel for as long as possible without orgasm. As the urge to climax begins to fade, you can go back to sexual thoughts. Then when you feel orgasm coming on again, you focus on your angel again. You can extend this for a very long time. With these simple instruction, using sexuality for mystical purposes should be very simple and enjoyable.

Awareness and Zen 13

I am neither a Zen master, nor do I think there is much to say about Zen. The Zen masters tell us that the more you say about Zen, the further you move away from the subject.

Many centuries ago, the wandering monk Bodhidharma brought Buddhism to China from India, and from there it traveled to Japan. The word *Zen* is a Japanese transliteration of the Sanskrit term *dhyana,* which we discussed in the chapter on yoga. To refresh your memory, dhyana is the state in which we are concentrating effortlessly upon a single object and it fills our whole consciousness. Zen is popularly thought of as conscious and effortless being in the flow of things. This description is not fully accurate, but again, it's a hard subject to define.

What I'm interested in briefly discussing is a technology that is not confined to Zen, but one that I happened to discover while I was studying Zen. This technology is "awareness." Awareness may not seem like a technology. You probably think you are aware right now. However, you are actually asleep in almost every way. For instance, until I mention it, you are probably not aware of the soles of your feet, or the surface that your butt is resting on, or the cling of your underwear upon your genitals. You're certainly not aware of the temperature of your left earlobe. You will of course become aware of these things momentarily as I bring them up, but they will quickly recede as you move on to other thoughts.

In actuality, we humans are almost never truly aware of anything. We perceive about one millionth of the available information around us. We see only those things that we expect to see, in as limited detail as our sleepwalking minds can muster. When we do finally become aware, we are enlightened. It is that simple.

The way that we become aware is also simple, although elusive. To become aware of something, you observe it without describing it, allowing yourself to experience it fully. This will at first be impossible, for immediately, your mind will wander. Eventually, you will fix your attention, and as you become fully aware of anything, you will become fully aware of the totality of yourself. In this totality, you will have the Knowledge and Conversation of your Holy Guardian Angel.

This technique can be used with anything. You could become aware of a blade of grass, or your hand, or your spine, or some chakra or energy center in your body. You could be aware of some person you love or some deity to which you are devoted. This technique is the secret behind mahasatipatthana.[1]

The key to this true awareness is to stop trying to describe your experience in reference to anything, and to experience it genuinely. When you do this, you are consciousness itself, the master who makes the grass green, and there is no mind and no body. There is only the ceaseless flow of life itself.

The Supreme Method 14

You may have noticed that all of the practices I have discussed have a number of things in common. All of them require concentration, and all of them carry you into an altered state of mind. The goal of all of these practices is the same: uniting your consciousness with that of the Holy Guardian Angel. Each of them takes a slightly different approach, and depending on your temperament or natural inclination, one or another of them may be most appropriate for you. Even a combination of the different techniques might be the best method for you—for instance, a yoga practice in the morning, and a magical ritual in the evening. There is no hard-and-fast rule, but there is one supreme method for the Knowledge and Conversation of your Holy Guardian Angel; it is, in fact, the true secret of the operation, and you can attain it with any of the practices I described in the previous chapters.

The supreme method for the Knowledge and Conversation of your Holy Guardian Angel is silence. Only in silence will you be able to hear the gentle whispers of your Angel and find him in the darkness. You cannot force silence to happen, it must simply come. All of the techniques that I have delineated can and will lead to this silence, but you must allow them to do so. If one or another of the techniques upsets or confounds you, it may not be appropriate for you to use at this time in your life.

When you begin to feel this silence, it may feel like emptiness. Do not fear, the darkness will soon break, and you will soon live in the divine light of your Angel. With this simple key, we can now move on to actually beginning your Abramelin operation.

PART III

Communion with the Divine

The Full Program 15

This chapter is for those of you who wish to follow every letter of the Abramelin operation. If you are using the Abramelin program as a model for designing a more personal program that fits your needs, I still recommend that you study this chapter. You may find that some of the instructions resonate with you. You may find them silly or repugnant. Many of the instructions are really quite practical, for example, "As for eating, drinking and sleeping, such should be in moderation and never superfluous." If you are not in control over these matters in your life, you will not likely be able to make a concentrated effort toward this operation. So, here are the instructions for the "orthodox" Abramelin operation.

As you begin the operation, you are supposed to give ten golden florins (and I have no idea what the exchange rate is these days) to the person who has given you this "Sacred

Magic," who is then supposed to split this up among seventy-two poor persons and have them recite the psalms, "Have Mercy upon me, O God. . ." and "Out of the Depths." Since no one has given you the "Sacred Magic," you will have to distribute these golden florins yourself. The charity seems to be symbolic of your commitment to the attainment of spiritual wealth, and a similar act of giving would probably do the trick. Once you have distributed the florins, you are ready to get started.

The First Two Months

In this first stage, you won't know at all what you're doing, but do not worry. Simply make sure that you go to your temple space and carry out your practices at the appointed times. The important thing at this stage is to avoid skipping your practices. Discipline and dedication are really what you should focus on, but here are the exact instructions:

> Every morning precisely a quarter of an hour before sunrise enter your Oratory, after having washed and dressed yourself in clean clothing, open the window, and then kneel at the Altar facing the window and invoke the Name of the Lord; after which you should confess to him your entire sins. This being finished you should supplicate Him that in time to come He may be willing and pleased to regard you with pity and grant you His grace and goodness to send unto you His Holy Angel, who shall serve unto you as a Guide. . . .[1]

> [At sunset, repeat the same invocation, confession, and prayer. During this first period, also observe the following rules:]

1. [Both the bed-chamber and oratory (working temple) are kept clean.] Your whole attention must be given to purity in all things.

2. You may sleep with your Wife in the bed when she is pure and clean.

3. [Every Saturday, change your bed sheets and perfume the chamber with incense.]

4. [Allow no animal to enter or dwell in the house, particularly in the bedchamber and your oratory.]

5. If you be your own Master, as far as lieth in your power, free yourself from all your business, and quit all mundane and vain company and conversation; leading a life tranquil, solitary and honest.

6. Take well heed in treating of business, in selling or buying, that it shall be requisite that you never give way unto anger, but be modest and patient in your actions.

7. You shall set apart two hours each day after having dined, during which you shall read with care the Holy Scripture and other Holy Books.

8. As for eating, drinking and sleeping, such should be in moderation and never superfluous.

9. Your dress should be clean but moderate, and according to custom. Flee all vanity.

10. As for that which regardeth the family, the fewer in number, the better; also act so that the servants may be modest and tranquil.

11. Let your hand be ever ready to give alms and other benefits to your neighbour; and let your heart be ever open unto the poor, whom God so loveth that one cannot express the same.[2]

The Second Two Months

During the second two months you are becoming more familiar with your practices, but at this stage you must make sure that you put even more passion into them, rather than allow them to become empty routines. They must still be carried out morning and evening. You must also observe the additional instruction:

> Before entering into the Oratory ye shall wash your hands and face thoroughly with pure water. And you shall prolong your prayer with the greatest possible affection, devotion and submission; humbly entreating the Lord God that he would deign to command His Holy Angels to lead you in the True Way. . . .

> [You should observe the following rules during this period:]

1. The use of the rites of Marriage is permitted, but should scarcely if at all be made use of.

2. You shall also wash your whole body every Sabbath Eve.

3. As to what regardeth commerce and rules of living, as in the first period.

4. It is absolutely necessary during this period to retire from the world and seek retreat.

5. Ye shall lengthen your prayers to the utmost of your ability.

6. As for eating, drinking, and clothing, as before."[3]

The Third Two Months

At this stage, you need to increase your practice to three times a day, and little else should be on your mind other than the operation. As much as possible, you should be in retirement from the world.

> Morning and Noon ye shall wash your hands and your face on entering the Oratory; and first ye shall make Confession of all your sins; after this, with a very ardent prayer, ye shall entreat the Lord to accord unto you this particular grace, which is, that you may enjoy and be able to endure the presence and conversation of His Holy Angels, and that He may deign by their inter-mission to grant unto you the Secret Wisdom, so that you may be able to have dominion over the Spirits and over all creatures. Ye shall do this same at midday before dining and also in the evening.[4]

[Here are the rules for the third two-month period:]

1. The man who is his own master shall leave all business alone, except works of charity towards his neighbour.

2. You shall shun all society except that of your Wife and of your Servants.

3. Ye shall employ the greatest part of your time in speaking of the Law of God.

4. Every Sabbath Eve shall ye fast, and wash your whole body, and change your garment.[5]

At the end of this period you finally will be ready to invoke your Angel.

Invoking Your Angel 16

Most of the techniques described in this book will help you invoke your Angel in a more natural way than described in the text of *The Abramelin*. However, if the path you are using to achieve your result is the devotional or the magical, you may wish to carry out the procedure outlined below. Understand that much of this material is metaphorical and refers to things that cannot be expressed with words.

On the morning following the completion of the third two months, "neither wash yourself at all nor dress yourself at all in your ordinary clothes; but take a Robe of Mourning; enter the Oratory with bare feet; go unto the side of the Censer, and having opened the windows, return unto the door. There prostrate yourself with your face against the ground."[1]

The Abramelin suggests you use a child as a clairvoyant assistant for the first part of this conjuration, but if you have used any of the techniques in this book, you will find your own abilities equal to or better than those of the average child. The child is supposed be between ages six and eight, and born in wedlock. The child is also supposed to be chosen before you begin the operation and is not supposed to know anything about the nature of it, lest he reveal it to the uninitiated. This all sounds rather dangerous to me in terms of the civil authorities, and it would be difficult to have a child keep the operation secret without that reflecting badly on you, should the child accidentally speak of it.

After you prostrate yourself on the ground, you "order the Child [or do it yourself] to put the Perfume upon the Censer, after which he is to place himself upon his knees before the Altar. . . ."[2]

Then, once all is in place, "Humiliate yourself before God and His Celestial Court, and commence your prayer with fervour, for then it is that you will begin to enflame yourself in praying, and you will see appear an extraordinary and supernatural Splendour which will fill the whole apartment [temple], and will surround you with an inexpressible odour, and this alone will console you and comfort your heart so that you shall call for ever happy the Day of the Lord."[3]

At this point, you or the child will ask the Angel to write, on a silver plate that you have already placed on the altar, a symbol or manner in which you can contact the Angel. Understand that this is symbolic; your angel will not "write" anything down. Rather, you will most likely gain the knowledge in a transcendental manner and write it down yourself. You will use it whenever you need your Angel.

You then leave the temple, and if you are using a child assistant, you let the child leave, as you no longer will have need of him or her. For the next three days, you will enter the temple and enjoy the Knowledge and Conversation of your Angel and all of the Good Angels, who will teach you unimaginable things. To quote Abramelin, "you shall see your Guardian Angel appear unto you in unequalled beauty: who also will converse with you, and speak in words so full of affection and of goodness, and with such sweetness, that no human tongue could express the same. . . . In one word, you shall be received by him with such affection that this description I here give unto you shall appear a mere nothing in comparison."[4]

For three days following the Knowledge and Conversation of your Angel, you will conjure the evil spirits and force them into obedience under your command. The next chapter deals with this stage.

Conquering the Four Evil Princes 17

The purpose of *The Abramelin* is to teach you a way to gain magical powers, but I have placed no emphasis on that throughout this book because the true goal of all goals is to attain the Knowledge and Conversation of the Holy Guardian Angel and the transcendental benefits of that experience. Giving undue prominence to the magical powers might lead you astray from the goal. However, you will gain extraordinary powers from the Abramelin operation.

When you have the knowledge of your Angel, you will have the attention of the highest authority in the universe. You will be a cocreator of your reality. You will have direct access to the part of your consciousness that determines your life experience. You will know your God.

By gaining the Knowledge and Conversation of the Holy Guardian Angel, you will have essentially conquered your mortal self and contacted that part of you that is immortal. You will no longer be subject to the same laws as you were before, or be the victim of fears, doubts, and delusions. You will still be vulnerable to those things, but you will have the ability to transcend them and rule them if you will it.

According to Abramelin, once you have received the Knowledge and Conversation of the Holy Guardian Angel, you must conjure a number of evil spirits and force them to swear an oath of obedience. As Aleister Crowley put it, "In the True Operation the Exaltation is equilibrated by an expansion in the other three arms of the Cross. Hence the Angel immediately gives the Adept power over the Four Great Princes and their servitors."[1] In transcendental terms, this means that you will have gained the ability to rise above the fears, doubts, and delusions of humanity. But you must still become their master by forcing them into obedience. "Every magician must firmly extend his empire to the depth of hell. 'My adepts stand upright, their heads above the heavens, their feet below the hells.' This is the reason why the magician who performs the Operation of the 'Sacred Magic of Abramelin the Mage,' immediately after attaining to the Knowledge and Conversation of the Holy Guardian Angel, must evoke the Four Great Princes of the Evil of the World."[2]

You may recall that these Four Great Princes, whose names are Lucifer, Leviathan, Satan, and Belial, are the personified powers of the four elemental fears that I discussed in chapter 5. The Princes' elemental correspondences are as follows:

Lucifer - Air

Leviathan - Fire

Satan - Water

Belial - Earth

I am not saying that evil spirits don't exist, or that they are mere figments of imagination. They certainly do exist, but they happen to be made of the doubts, fears, and delusions of humanity. You could also say that the doubts, fears, and delusions of humanity are made of demons.

Whether you conquer the demons of fear with a ceremony, by a process of introspection, or by shouting them down, you must conquer these forces in your life. If you do not, you will find yourself slowly falling under their thrall once more, and you will lose sight of your Angel once again in the mire of worldly fears and pains.

The matter of how to properly conjure the evil spirits and how to gain their servitude will certainly be clear to you once you have the Knowledge and Conversation of your Angel, but I'd like to point out a few things. When you conjure them, you must force them to swear obedience to you on the point of your wand, which is a magical representation of your will. The conjurations of the evil spirits generally last for three days. On the first day, you conjure the Four Great Princes, Lucifer, Leviathan, Satan, and Belial; on the second day you conjure the Eight Lesser Princes, Astarot, Magot, Asmodee, Belzebud, Oriens, Paimon, Ariton, and Amaimon; and on the third day you conjure their many Servitors. When addressing any spirit, you should be polite and courteous but commanding. These devils are only frightening if you allow yourself to be their slave. Actually, you are the creator and ruler of these demons of fear. This is the great irony of most Christians' fears about the Devil. Anyone who is connected with God has no reason whatsoever to fear any devils.

The specific manner in which you contact the spirits and how they will manifest is up to you and your Angel. I used a technique similar to Goetic conjuration and conjured each spirit in turn in a triangular magick mirror. This method was completely of my own devising, and you may find some other much more suitable to you.

Interestingly, I made the spirits give me a symbol with which I could command and control them. I later realized that *The Lesser Key of Solomon* names several of the spirits in this operation, along with an illustration of their symbols, or sigils. I compared the symbols I received with those in *The Lesser Key of Solomon,* and I discovered that they were very congruent; a couple of them were startlingly so. None were exactly the same, but that doesn't surprise me at all.

The ritual outlines of the ceremonies I performed to conjure the evil spirits are listed below. They are suggestions, and I do not recommend that you follow them exactly. Also, the attribution of Lucifer to Air, Leviathan to Fire, Satan to Water, and Belial to Earth is my own, which I based on my intuitions and instructions from my Angel. Anton La Vey suggests in his *Satanic Bible*[3] these alternate attributions: Lucifer to Air, Leviathan to Water, Satan to Fire, and Belial to Earth. You may agree with these more, since Leviathan is sometimes referred to as a sea serpent. To me, he is a fiery dragon. You may find that none of these attributions work for you at all. Trust yourself.

DAY 1- Conjuration of the Four Evil Princes

Preparation

Banishing

Perform the Lesser Banishing Ritual of the Pentagram (see page 91).

PURIFICATION

I purify myself with water Adonai; may I be purified to accomplish this work in perfection.

CONSECRATION

I consecrate myself with fire; Adonai, may I have the strength to accomplish this spell with power.

OATH

*I stand at the center of the Wheel; I reach out beyond the edges of infinity. I stand before my light-transcending Mother, within me the source of All, and without me every power in heaven and below the Earth, to invoke the Four Evil Princes that rule the powers of the world and under the world, **Lucifer, Leviathan, Satan, Belial.** Because it is the will of God, my Holy Guardian Angel, and all of the heavens, I shall succeed this day.*

PRELIMINARY INVOCATION

The preliminary invocation that I use is very powerful for me, but each person should compose an invocation that is personally meaningful. After your invocaton, you must relax your consciousness into a visionary state. Using repetition along with bodily relaxation will bring you easily into the right state of mind.

Lucifer - Air

I invoke you, Lucifer; you are the fears of my intellect. Oh rebellious spirit, you have refused repeatedly to submit to discipline. You chatter endlessly, and you are a slave master. You have allowed me to think only certain thoughts and have made it difficult for me to think others. You have made mathematics strenuous for me. You have tricked me into thinking I am using logic as I have bowed in slavery to one of your fellow demons. You have told me I am not intelligent enough, that my decisions are incorrect, and that I am insane. You've given me an inability to draw conclusions, and made me stuck in overthinking things.

*I demand your appearance that you may give me the power of **knowledge and logic** in the name of my Angel and in the name of all the powers of the universe. Lucifer, Lucifer, Lucifer, Lucifer, Lucifer, Lucifer.* [While chanting, visualize a demon with the airy qualities described above appearing before you.]

Lucifer, you have made me describe things with words, images, and thoughts. I have foolishly allowed you to influence these thoughts. From now on, I will use my thoughts to empower me, always seeking more light. From now on, I will rule the affairs of my mind and all of the affairs that you govern, I command you to submit yourself to my will, and I present to you my wand. As a show of good faith, I command that you give me the seal by which you are commanded and controlled.

From now on, I will have knowledge. I will enjoy logic and problem-solving skills.

Leviathan - Fire

I invoke you, Leviathan; you are the fears of my passion. Oh fiery serpent of the abysmal, you have fooled me into thinking that I know things that I do not know, and that I cannot know things that I do. You have made me question my own power, and you have crippled my ability to act. You have

*fooled me into thinking in terms of good and evil and have
rotted my brain with moral strictures. You have made me fear
my passions. You have enslaved me with lust and then made
me feel guilty about my desires.*

*I demand your appearance that you may give me the
power of **personal will and passion** in the name of my Angel
and in the name of all the powers of the Universe. Leviathan,
Leviathan, Leviathan, Leviathan, Leviathan, Leviathan.*
[While chanting, visualize a demon with the fiery qualities
described above appearing before you.]

*Leviathan, you have fooled me into believing in morals
and codes that I did not choose. From now on, I will be the
master of my beliefs, and I will choose empowering beliefs
that free me from all slavery. I will have true personal power.
From now on, I will rule the affairs of my will and passion
and all of the affairs that you govern. I command you to submit yourself to my will, and I present to you my wand. As a
show of good faith I command that you give me the seal by
which you are commanded and controlled.*

*From now on, I will have passion. I will enjoy the power
and will to make decisions, and carry through with them.*

Satan - Water

*I invoke you, Satan; you are the fears of my emotions. Oh
tempting spirit, you have tricked me into projecting my feelings onto others. You have twisted my intuition into a parody
of fear. You have driven me to feel poorly about myself and
to be afraid of my own feelings. You have tricked me into
submitting foolishly to the wills of others. You have made me
overly concerned about what others think of me, afraid of
love and friendship, and have given me feelings of loneliness.*

*I demand your appearance that you may give me the power of **fame and intuition** in the name of my Angel and in the name of all the powers of the universe. Satan, Satan, Satan, Satan, Satan, Satan, Satan.* [While chanting, visualize a demon with the watery qualities described above appearing before you.]

Satan, you have fooled me into looking for approval from the outside. You have made me seek acceptance in the pack hierarchy. You have fooled me into thinking that others determine my status in the tribe. I strike out from this lie. In fact, I alone control my state. From now on, I will only look to myself for all questions of behavior and I will rule my own emotions. I will rule the affairs of my heart and all of the affairs that you govern. I command you to submit yourself to my will, and I present to you my wand. As a show of good faith, I command that you give me the seal by which you are commanded and controlled.

From now on, I will have fame. I will enjoy intuition, and control over my emotional body.

Belial - Earth

I invoke you, Belial; you are the fears of my body. Oh dishonest spirit, you have lied to me through my eyes, telling me falsehoods that have made me fearful of my fellow humans. You have fooled me into seeing things the same way over and over again. You have stolen my spontaneity. You have hidden the truth from me on countless occasions, blocking my eyes. You have tried to give me anxiety about money, and you have whispered fearful thoughts about health into my ears. You have made me hate my body and encouraged me to mistreat it. You have long sought to ruin my physical well-being. You have given me hundreds of ills and injuries throughout my life. You try to stop my progress in life by making me weary.

*I demand your appearance that you may give me the power of **wealth and health** in the name of my Angel and in the name of all the powers of the universe. Belial, Belial, Belial, Belial, Belial, Belial.* [While chanting, visualize a demon with the earthy qualities described above appearing before you.]

Belial, you have tried to trick me about seeking those things that are pleasant and avoiding those that are unpleasant. From now on, I will decide consciously what is pleasant and what is unpleasant and know that I can make any unpleasant experience into a pleasant one by changing my frame of reference. From now on, I will rule the affairs of my body and all of the affairs that you govern. I command you to submit yourself to my will, and I present to you my wand. As a show of good faith, I command that you give me the seal by which you are commanded and controlled.

From now on, I will have wealth. I will enjoy mechanical dexterity and physical affection.

Closing

DISMISSAL

Perform the License to Depart. *Oh spirits, because you have diligently answered my demands, I license you to depart unto your abodes. Depart, withdrawing peacefully, ready to return at my command.*

BANISHING

Perform the Lesser Banishing Ritual of the Pentagram (see page 91).

DAY 2- Conjuration of the Eight Sub-Princes

Preparation

BANISHING

Perform the Lesser Banishing Ritual of the Pentagram (see page 91).

PURIFICATION

I purify myself with water; Adonai, may I be purified to accomplish this work in perfection.

CONSECRATION

I consecrate myself with fire; Adonai, may I have the strength to accomplish this spell with power.

OATH

*I stand at the center of the Wheel; I reach out beyond the edges of infinity. I stand before my light-transcending Mother, within me the source of All, and without me every power in heaven and below the Earth, to invoke the Eight Sub-princes who rule under the Four Evil Princes. They are **Astarot, Magot, Asmodee, Belzebud, Oriens, Paimon, Ariton, Amaimon.** Because it is the will of God, my Holy Guardian Angel, and all of the heavens, I shall succeed this day.*

PRELIMINARY INVOCATION

Perform your own invocation and get into a visionary state.

Conjuration

By the power of my Holy Guardian Angel, and by the power of the Four Evil Princes Lucifer, Leviathan, Satan, and Belial,

I conjure you Eight Sub-princes of the Dark Realms. I conjure you each by name.

Astarot, ruler of communication in general and destruction in particular, I conjure you, Astarot, Astarot, Astarot.

Magot, ruler of magical force in general and blocking in particular, I conjure you, Magot, Magot, Magot.

Asmodee, ruler of lust, debauch in general and secret knowledge in particular, I conjure you.

Belzebud, ruler of physical force in general and anger in particular, I conjure you.

Oriens, ruler of the East and intellectual ability in general and creating wealth in particular, I conjure you.

Paimon, ruler of the South and ferocity in general and war in particular, I conjure you.

Ariton, ruler of the West and intuition in general and the discovery of theft in particular, I conjure you.

Amaimon, ruler of the North and healing of diverse maladies in general and particular, I conjure you.

From now on, I will rule all of the affairs that you govern, I command you to submit yourself to my will and I present to you my wand. What I ask for from you with the talismanic symbols of Abramelin or any other command, I will receive, by your power or the power of your inferior spirits. As a show of good faith, I command that you each in turn give me the seal by which you are commanded and controlled.

Closing

DISMISSAL

Perform the License to Depart. *Oh spirits, because you have diligently answered my demands, I license you to depart unto your abodes. Depart, withdrawing peacefully, ready to return at my command.*

Banishing

Perform the Lesser Banishing Ritual of the Pentagram (see page 91).

DAY 3- Conjuration of the Evil Spirits

Preparation

Banishing

Perform the Lesser Banishing Ritual of the Pentagram (see page 91).

Purification

I purify myself with water; Adonai, may I be purified to accomplish this work in perfection.

Consecration

I consecrate myself with fire; Adonai, may I have the strength to accomplish this spell with power.

Oath

I stand at the center of the Wheel, I reach out beyond the edges of infinity. I stand before my light-transcending Mother, within me the source of All, and without me every power in heaven and below the Earth, to invoke the Many Spirits who are the executors of magick under the Eight Sub-princes who rule under the Four Evil Princes. Because it is the will of God,

my Holy Guardian Angel, and all of the heavens, I shall suc-
ceed this day.

PRELIMINARY INVOCATION

Perform your own invocation and get into a visionary state.

Conjuration

By the Power of My Holy Guardian Angel, and by the power of
the Four Evil Princes, Lucifer, Leviathan, Satan, and Belial; and
the Eight Sub-princes, Astarot, Magot, Asmodee, Belzebud,
Oriens, Paimon, Ariton, and Amaimon, I conjure you, Many
Spirits of the Dark Realms. I conjure you each by name.

[I then listed all the 316 spirits in *The Abramelin* on pages
105–109.]

By the power of my Holy Guardian Angel, and by the power
of the Four Evil Princes, Lucifer, Leviathan, Satan, and Belial;
and the Eight Sub-princes, Astarot, Magot, Asmodee, Belzebud,
Oriens, Paimon, Ariton, and Amaimon, I command you, Many
Spirits of the Dark Realms. From now on, I will rule all of the
affairs that you govern, I command you to submit yourself to my
will, and I present to you my wand. What I ask for from you
with the talismanic symbols of Abramelin or any other command,
I will receive, by your power or the power of your inferior spirits.

Closing

DISMISSAL

Perform the License to Depart. *Oh spirit, because you have*
diligently answered my demands, I license you to depart unto

your abodes. Depart, withdrawing peacefully, ready to return at my command.

BANISHING

Perform the Lesser Banishing Ritual of the Pentagram (see page 91).

The Abramelin Squares 18

The Abramelin squares form a sort of "practical magick" that you use after the conclusion of your operation. Many students, when looking into the Abramelin operation, become absolutely fascinated by the huge collection of lettered magical squares in the back of *The Abramelin*. The magician uses these squares to command the spirits, and they are supposed to signal to the spirits whatever wonderful effects you want to achieve. With one look at the squares, you can understand how they could fascinate a person. Each of the squares is used for a different magical effect, and many possible magical desires have a square. With these squares, a magician can do anything, from creating armies and vast fortunes to visions of operas and unicorns. Unfortunately, some students become obsessed with the magic squares, and all they want to do is figure out how to use them.

The squares are a series of lettered acrostics or sometimes just random sets of letters. Some of the letters seem related to words, while others seem completely untranslatable. They are written in a strange kind of magical gibberish. This gibberish is the language of dreams, the language of spirits and magick. There is no way to rationally explain or define the symbols. Until you are able to speak this language fluently, the squares will be useless to you. This language can only be learned from communication with your Angel.

S. L. MacGregor Mathers, the 19th-century ceremonial magician, translator and editor of *The Abramelin,* attempted to make connections between the words on the squares and various Hebrew, Chaldean, Greek, and Latin words and roots. In many cases, a relationship does seem to exist, and in others it is rather dubious. Mathers himself admits to making guesses in many cases.

The squares are broken up into 30 categories of Magical Effect:

1. To Know all Manner of Things Past and Future, Which be not However Directly Opposed to God, and to His Most Holy Will.

2. To Obtain Information Concerning, and to be Enlightened upon all sorts of Propositions and all Doubtful Sciences.

3. To Cause any Spirit to appear, and take any form, such as of Man, Animal, Bird, etc.

4. For divers Visions.

5. How We May Retain the Familiar Spirits Bond or Free in Whatever Form.

6. To Cause Mines to be Pointed Out, and to Help Forward all kinds of Work Connected Therewith.

7. To Cause the Spirits to Perform with Facility and Promptitude all Necessary Chemical Labours and Operations, as Regardeth Metals Especially.

8. To Excite Tempests.

9. To Transform Animals into Men, and Men into Animals; etc.

10. To Hinder any Necromantic or Magical Operations from Taking Effect, except those of the Qabala and of this Sacred Magic.

11. To Cause all Kinds of Books to be Brought to One, and Whether Lost or Stolen.

12. To Know the Secrets of any Person.

13. To Cause a Dead Body to Revive, and Perform all the Functions Which a Living Person Would do, and this during a Space of Seven Years, by Means of the Spirits.

14. The Twelve Symbols for the hours of the Day and of the Night, to render oneself Invisible to every person.

15. For the Spirits.

16. To Find and Take Possession of all kinds of Treasures, provided that they be not at all (Magically) guarded.

17. To Fly in the Air and Travel any Whither.

18. To Heal Divers Maladies.

19. For Every Description of Affection and Love.

20. To Excite every Description of Hatred and Enmity, Discords, Quarrels, Contentions, Combats, Battles, Loss, and Damage.

21. To Transform Oneself, and take Different Faces and Forms.

22. These are Only for Evil, for with the Symbols Herein we can Cast Spells, and Work Every Kind of Evil; We should not Avail Ourselves hereof.

23. To Demolish Buildings and Strongholds.

24. To Discover any Thefts that Hath Occured.

25. To Walk Upon, and Operate Under, Water.

26. To Open every kind of Lock, without a Key, and without making any Noise.

27. To Cause Visions to Appear.

28. To Have as much Gold and Silver as one may wish, both to Provide for one's Necessities, and to Live in Opulence.

29. To Cause Armed Men to Appear.

30. To Cause Comedies, Operas, and every kind of Music and Dances to appear.[1]

Many of these magical effects seem rather silly and impractical. I had originally intended to publish the magical squares as an appendix at the end of this book, but there was always a strange nagging at the back of my mind whenever I'd think about it. I consulted deeply with my own Holy Guardian Angel and decided that I did not want to include the squares in this book. The truly important magick described in this book is the union with your Angel. Compared to that experience, all of the powers of these squares are mere trifles. I did not want to distract from or muddle this singular message.

However, I do want to make a few comments about the Abramelin squares. I want to emphasize that you use the squares only *after* you have attained the Knowledge and Conversation of your Holy Guardian Angel, and *after* you have gained the obedience of the evil spirits. Before having accomplished these things, the squares are useless, or worse than useless. They are purported to be dangerous. There are many rumors about people going crazy and getting injured or killed by trying to use the squares without going through the full operation. I must interject the suggestion that these people were probably pretty unbalanced from the beginning. The spirits of the squares probably didn't have that much work to do, but you would still be wise to avoid the temptation to play around with the Abramelin squares.

In reality, the Abramelin squares are mostly just variations on Hebrew, Chaldeic, and Greek words that express the effect they are intended to produce. They are like crib sheets that tell the spirits what you want. They often do not literally translate into the exact effect, but rather allude to it in strange and sometimes hypnotizing ways. The squares are written in the language of the unconscious, the language of Magick and Spirits. Until you speak that language, the letters and squares will do you no good. It is only once we have the transcendent experience of our Angel that we may fully understand the message of the squares. This message is individual, and the magick that you perform will be entirely different from the magick that I perform. This is simply the way that the universe works. The Abramelin squares may or may not become a part of your magick.

If you would like to use these symbols, you are supposed to prepare them before the Abramelin operation, and keep them wrapped in a safe place until you have attained your Angel and the submission of the Evil Spirits. There is no need to concern yourself with "magic ink" or "virgin parchment" when making these squares according to Abramelin. You need only draw them on paper to seek the desired results. Using these symbols is an art as much as any other art, and you cannot expect to raise tempests the first time you try. The instructions for using the squares entail holding the appropriate square in your hand and saying what you want.

Even if you never use the Abramelin squares themselves, you will find your life shifting into new territory when you complete this operation. You will find yourself able to change all of the conditions of your life simply by contacting your source. You will be able to attract all those things into your life that you need and want. Your past fears, desires, and pains will slowly fade, and you will gradually awaken into the celestial and all-powerful being that you truly are.

You will not, however, be able to do just anything or everything you feel like. You will need to consult your Angel before using your power in any way. Your Angel will allow into your life all the miracles that you really need—and no others. In truth, your Angel will help you become the greatest being you could ever hope to become. And with that, our paths must at last part, but it is fitting to let the words of Abramelin bid you farewell:

"At this point I commence to restrict myself in my writing, seeing that by the Grace of the Lord I have submitted and consigned you unto a MASTER so great that he will never let you err."[2]

Notes

Introduction

1 Please read "The Wake World," in Aleister Crowley's small book of essays, *Konx Om Pax* (Chicago: Teitan Press, 1990), for a colorful depiction of the spiritual process as the relation between Natural Soul and Holy Guardian Angel.

2 Aleister Crowley, *Magick: Book Four, Liber ABA* (York Beach, ME: Weiser, 1997), p. 260. Further references to this book will be cited as *Magick*.

3 Israel Regardie, *The Tree of Life* (York Beach, ME: Weiser, 1995), p. 196.

4 Crowley, *Magick*, p. 494.

Chapter 1

1 Please don't mistake love for sentimentality or weakness. Real love is a fierce thing. Love allows things that must end to die, and it looks at suffering without blinking. Love is an extension toward unity, not a prison or something that can be expressed with a greeting card.

2 Aleister Crowley, *Magick Without Tears* (Tempe, AZ: New Falcon, 1994), pp. 281–282.

3 Crowley, *Magick*, p. 494.

4 S. L. MacGregor Mathers, trans., *The Book of the Sacred Magic of Abramelin the Mage* (New York: Dover, 1975), p. 74.

5 Aleister Crowley, *The Vision and the Voice: The Equinox vol. 4, no. 2* (York Beach, ME: Weiser, 1997), p. 179. This is the official A∴ A∴ instruction for obtaining the Knowledge and Conversation of the Holy Guardian Angel.

Chapter 2

1 Crowley, *Magick,* pp. 234–235.

2 Abramelin suggests that you enter your temple twice a day at sunrise and sunset, but just once a day will probably be sufficient in the beginning. You could, of course, go for two times if you're a trooper, but this is hard to do immediately, and you don't want to fail right at the outset.

3 Prayer can be considered any attempt to reach out to the universe. Meditation, ritual, dance, these are all prayers if done in a sincere effort to reach up toward the heavens. In this day and age, "confessing your sins" should not be taken quite as literally as it was written. See chapter 4 for a discussion on the true nature and significance of confession.

4 Mathers, *Abramelin*, p. 65.

Chapter 3

1 Mathers, *Abramelin*, p. 54.

2 Ibid., p. 64

3 Crowley, *Magick*, p. 60.

4 Such as robes, altars, wands, etc.

5 This wand is for conjuring and commanding the evil spirits. Before you can truly be an illumined being, you must conquer these evil spirits even if it is in a less ceremonious way than described in the text. See chapter 17.

Chapter 4

1 Mathers, *Abramelin*, p. 88.

2 Ibid., p. 65.

3 Crowley, *Magick*, p. 238.

4 Mathers, *Abramelin*, p. 81

5 J. F. C. Fuller, "The Temple of Solomon the King" in Aleister Crowley et al., *The Equinox*, vol. 1, no. 3 (York Beach, ME: Weiser, 1992), p. 244. A student of Aleister Crowley's, Fuller wrote several books about Crowley and his work and is also known for his many books on military strategy.

6 Miguel de Molinos, *The Spiritual Guide Which Disentangles the Soul* (London: Methuen, 1950), p. 103.

7 Crowley, *Magick,* p. 231.

8 Kundalini Shakti is the goddess who is said to live in the base (muladhara) chakra of the spine. She is in the form of a sleeping serpent coiled three and a half times around an egg. Her awakening is the beginning of cosmic consciousness and power.

9 *Hadit* is the infinite yet omnipresent point, and *Nuit* is infinite space. These terms are used in Thelema, which is the philosophy that Aleister Crowley received in T*he Book of the Law.*

10 "Liber Al Vel Legis," I, line 61, in Aleister Crowley, *The Book of the Law* (York Beach, ME: Weiser, 1989), p. 27.

11 Mathers, *Abramelin,* p. 64.

12 Scientific Remote Viewing is the practice of sensing unseen information by using a set of regulated protocols.

13 de Molinos, *The Spiritual Guide,* p. 124.

14 King James Bible, Mark 10:15.

15 de Molinos, *The Spiritual Guide*, p. 198.

16 Mathers, *Abramelin*, p. 66.

17 de Molinos, *The Spiritual Guide*, p. 98.

18 You could take *The Abramelin*'s instruction literally, although rather than purifying you, it would most likely result in you dwelling in your own filth. This could be helpful in retiring from other people, as they would be avoiding you!

19 de Molinos, *The Spiritual Guide*, p. 124.

20 Crowley, *Magick*, p. 269.

21 Ibid.

Chapter 5

1 These notions still apply in Freudian psychology, where you see earth in the "id," water in the "subconscious," air in the "ego," and fire in the "superego."

2 Robert Anton Wilson, *Prometheus Rising* (Tempe, AZ: New Falcon, 1983), p. 162. See also Timothy Leary, *The Game of Life* (Tempe, AZ: New Falcon, 1993).

3 "Liber Al vel Legis," I, line 3, in Aleister Crowley, *The Book of the Law* (York Beach, ME: Weiser, 1989), p. 19.

4 de Molinos, *The Spiritual Guide*, p. 73.

Chapter 6

1 J. F. C. Fuller, "Temple of Solomon the King," in Crowley et al., *The Equinox,* vol. 1, no. 3 (York Beach, ME: Weiser, 1992), p. 244.

Chapter 7

1 Crowley, *Magick,* p. 37.

2 Swami Vivekananda, *Raja-Yoga, Jnana-Yoga,* and *Karma-Yoga and Bhakti–Yoga* (New York: Ramakrishna Vivekananda Center, 1982).

3 *Eight Lectures on Yoga, The Equinox, Magick,* and *Magick Without Tears.*

4 "Prana" is also a name for a pervasive spiritual energy that fills the universe, and mastery of pranayama means mastery of this hidden energy. This is what gives yogis their siddhis, or magical powers. The word for breath and spirit are the same in many cultures: pneuma (Greek), ruach (Hebrew), spiritus, and chi (Chinese), just to name a few.

5 The more hedonistic Westerner will probably prefer going into deep relaxation by sitting in an easy chair or lying on the floor, which can have the same results. The danger in this case is falling asleep instead of feeling pain.

Chapter 8

1 A comprehensive list of these magical correspondences can be found in Crowley, *777 and Other Qabalistic Writings*. (York Beach, ME: Weiser, 1988).

2 The circle openings in most forms of modern witchcraft are another excellent example of this sort of banishing ritual.

3 See "Liber O vel Manus et Sagittae," in Crowley, *Magic*, p. 618, for Crowley's version of this ritual.

4 Crowely, *Magic*, p. 692

5 See "Liber Samekh" in Crowely, *Magic*, pp. 513–541 for Crowley's own version of this ritual.

6 See "Liber O vel Manus et Sagittæ," in Crowley, *Magic*, pp. 613–626

Chapter 9

1 This should not be taken to mean Christians only. There are those whose enthusiasm devolves into empty, mindless bigotry in every religious persuasion.

2 In Crowley's "Liber O" (cited in chapter 8, note 3), you will find more information on astral projection and rising on the planes.

Chapter 10

1   This is the Akashic Egg, which is the Indian Tattwa symbol that corresponds to the Western mystical concept of the spirit element. In many cultures, the egg is an archetypal symbol of the spiritual body and the universe.

Chapter 11

1   Crowley, *Magick*, p. 628.

Chapter 12

1   Louis Culling, *A Manual of Sex Magick* (St. Paul, MN: Llewellyn, 1989), p. 18.

Chapter 13

1   This is the Buddhist breathing technique of mentally following the breath as it comes in and goes out.

Chapter 14

No notes.

Chapter 15

1   Mathers, *Abramelin*, p. 64. Some of the following quotations have been abridged.

2 Ibid., pp. 66–69.

3 Ibid., pp. 69, 70.

4 Ibid., pp. 70, 71.

5 Ibid., p. 71.

Chapter 16

1 Mathers, *Abramelin,* p. 81.

2 Ibid.

3 Ibid.

4 Ibid., p. 84.

Chapter 17

1 Crowley, *Magick,* p. 275.

2 Ibid., p. 278.

3 Anton La Vey, *The Satanic Bible* (New York: William Morrow, 1972), pp. 27, 37, 107, 141.

Chapter 18

1 Mathers, *Abramelin,* pp. 136–138.

2 Ibid., p. 85.

Bibliography

Crowley, Aleister. *The Book of the Law.* York Beach, ME: Weiser, 1989.

———. *Eight Lectures on Yoga.* Tempe, AZ: New Falcon, 1992.

———. *Konx Om Pax.* Des Moines, IA: Yoga Publication Society, 1973.

———. *Magick: Book Four, Liber ABA.* (York Beach, ME: Weiser, 1997.

———. *Magick Without Tears.*, Tempe, AZ: New Falcon, 1994.

———. *777 and other Qabalistic Writings.* York Beach, ME: Weiser, 1988.

———. *The Vision and the Voice: The Equinox* vol. 4, no. 2. York Beach, ME: Weiser, 1997.

Crowley, Aleister et al., *The Equinox,* vols. 1–10. York Beach, ME: Weiser, 1992.

Culling, Louis. *A Manual of Sex Magick.* St Paul, MN: Llewellyn, 1989.

Fuller, J. F. C. "Temple of Solomon the King," in Aleister Crowley et al., *The Equinox,* vol. 1, no. 3. York Beach, ME: Weiser, 1992.

Leary, Timothy. *The Game of Life.* Tempe, AZ: New Falcon, 1993.

Mathers, S. L. Macgregor, trans. *The Book of the Sacred Magic of Abramelin the Mage.* New York: Dover, 1975.

Molinos, Miguel de. *The Spiritual Guide Which Disentangles the Soul.* London: Methuen, 1950.

Regardie, Israel. *The Tree of Life.* York Beach, ME: Weiser, 1995.

Wilson, Robert Anton. *Prometheus Rising* Tempe, AZ: New Falcon, 1983.